Cacti

Ward Lock Ltd, London

Cacti

by Sir Oliver Leese Bt

Acknowledgments

The photographs in this book were supplied by the author, with the exception of the following illustrations:
Spectrum Colour Library (photographed at Worfield Gardens, Bridgnorth, Shropshire, England) 50, 54, 55bl&r, 57tr,b, 58, 59, 60l,tr, 62t, 63tl,bl&r, 65, 66, 67, 69tr, 70t,bl, 74, 75, 78t, 109t, 120, 122t, 123c, 127, 134, 136, 137tr,bl, 140
Spectrum Colour Library 10, 41, 51t, 63tr, 68, 71, 77, 79br, 191, 102, 103, 104, 121, 124b, 125, 141

ISBN 0 7063 1121 3
Published by
Ward Lock Limited
Designed and produced by
Trewin Copplestone Publishing Ltd, London
© Trewin Copplestone Publishing Ltd 1973
Printed in Great Britain by
Sir Joseph Causton & Sons Ltd
London & Eastleigh

Contents

Preface

As I have been lucky enough to visit many of the countries where cactus and succulent plants grow in the wild, I have tried to pass on the knowledge I have gained. The section of this book called 'In their natural habitat', and the photographs which I took on these expeditions, may therefore add to the interest of growing one's own collection, for all who lack the opportunity to observe these plants growing in the wild.

I have also tried to present in simple and understandable form all the information needed by the novice collector. If more technical details are required, readers may find it useful to refer to my book *Desert Plants,* which was published more than ten years ago. It is now out of print and will not be re-published, but it should be possible to consult copies in public libraries.

This book has been written in the northern hemisphere, and readers in the southern hemisphere –from South Africa, Australia or New Zealand– may be a little confused, as the references to summer and winter are at totally different times of the year to those with which they are accustomed. For instance, the best time to see spring flowers in South Africa is in September and October. But the principles are just the same. In the spring and summer plants like plenty of water and sunshine. Plants indoors are liable to get drawn and yellow if they do not have enough sunlight. Some plants like some shade from the merciless midday sun especially in days of drought.

I welcome this opportunity to thank those who have helped me so much with this book. Frances Denby for all her encouragement, without which I would never have taken on another book, and for her help and guidance on the countries we have both visited. Some of the photographs were taken by her and she has helped with the selection of the best photographs to use. Barbara Randall, who has given so much of her spare time to preparing the final text of the whole book. To Esther Reiss, for her help in checking the nomenclature, and to Alfred Randall for his help and advice on the care and cultivation of succulents.

The author in action in the Pretoria Botanical Gardens

The author near Tucson with a very old Ferocactus Wislezenii which was leaning so perilously towards the sun that a few years later it fell

What are cacti and succulent plants?

A collection of cacti and other succulent plants can be a great thrill to people of all ages, occupations and interests, and the object of this book is to develop this hobby and to bring its fascination within the reach of many. It is already a thriving hobby — and a most friendly one. Numerous societies the whole world over exist to help enthusiasts to get together regularly in organized groups to exchange experiences and material. The amount of international good-will generated and sustained by such activities would surprise quite a few politicians.

I believe that we can go a long way towards understanding our plants if we study their habits and way of life in their countries of origin, and then try to imitate some of these conditions in the manner in which we display and cultivate our own plants here. Any information so gleaned must, of course, be modified to suit the circumstances in which we have to grow our plants, and these vary considerably. The first few chapters of this book deal with the manner in which plants grow in their natural habitats in America and Africa, and later chapters will suggest methods by which some of these conditions can be adapted to those in which our plants have to live in our homes in more northern countries. There are also descriptions of plants which are particularly recommended for starting a collection.

With over 9000 plants to choose from, one obviously has to be highly selective in picking out here and there examples which one considers to be of particular value to various kinds of people, whether established collectors, or beginners, or bowl garden enthusiasts, or those who want plants which are fairly easy to flower.

If one is lucky enough to be able to examine indigenous plants at first hand in the wild, so much the better. Those who are not fortunate enough to do this can get great pleasure and interest from seeing them in countries in which they are bedded out.

Some of you will by now be saying to yourselves 'What exactly is a succulent plant? And is it correct that a cactus belongs to the same group?' Then you will be asking if it is true that all the 'spiny ones' are cacti, and that they bloom only once in every seven years? These and many other questions I hope to answer, starting with the reply to those two most provocative questions. 'What is a succulent?' and 'What is the difference between cacti and other succulents?' How many times have I been asked this! The trouble is that the term 'succulent' is an arbitrary one commonly applied to a very large group of plants, all of which have it in common that they can for varying periods withstand drought conditions.

Some people expect to find these plants only in arid deserts, and it is well at this stage to correct the mis-conception about deserts and the plants that grow there. True deserts support practically no vegetation at all. In the perfect geographical sense of the word, a desert lacks life almost completely. It is in situations more appropriately described as 'scrub' 'karoo' 'semi-desert' or 'prairie' that our succulent plants abound. They can store varying amounts of moisture which enable them to tide over long dry periods, during which the roots may absorb little if any moisture from the soil. During the rains, water intake may be considerable, and an emergency store of moisture is built up in stems, plant body, leaves or rootstock. Some plants further help themselves to survive the dry season by settling down to low activity, almost like a hibernating animal.

The history of succulents, in common with that of other plants, is still largely a matter of conjecture. Fossils of plants, unlike those of animals, are relatively rare, and we cannot tell with any degree of accuracy when succulents began to develop. Their beginning must have been coupled with the development of desert conditions, and there have been deserts on earth for much of its history, though the deserts of today are, geologically speaking, relatively recent, most of them having come into being during the last fifteen million years, in conjunction with the steady uplift of the mountains we know today.

The presence of mountains has created several present-day deserts, because moisture-bearing winds deposit their moisture as they pass over high ranges, with the result that areas of very low rainfall occur on the leeward sides. Just being a long way from the sea may cause an area to be a desert, for winds from the sea tend to lose moisture as they blow further and further inland. Deserts are to be found especially in two bands parallel with the Equator, north and south of it, and often on the western sides of continents, because the movement of the main winds are themselves controlled by the ocean currents.

In these belts of high atmospheric pressure, frequent gusty winds, alternating with periods of dead calm, allow little rain either to form or fall. What little does fall is normally in short, heavy summer thunderstorms. Within these belts on either side of the Equator, and usually behind mountains, the 'desert' lands have been created. Erosion is caused either by the wind or by periodical raging torrents. Vegetation and humus have been swept away, rocks have fallen from the mountain sides and vast areas of sand and rock have been formed. Sometimes deserts are flat, but often they are undulating and sometimes mountainous with a landscape varying from the wind-swept sand dunes of the Sahara to the salt flats of North America. When the longed-for rains come, torrential rivers tear across the sunbaked ground, carving out deep canyons in place of the broad river beds which can only exist where there are frequent and soft rains. Whether the succulents evolved from plants which originally grew in these areas before they became deserts, or whether they evolved from plants which gradually colonized desert areas, we may never discover. Suffice it to say that over the epochs, a desert flora, common curiously enough to America, Africa and Asia, came into being, and that some plants which lived in the areas of longest drought cast off their branches and leaves and retained little except their 'bodies', as in the majority of the cacti.

Many of the cactus plants have the most strange shapes which, while bearing little resemblance to other flower-bearing plants in the world today, can nevertheless produce lovely flowers. They have apparently discarded their branches and twigs and reduced them to spines, and either diminished their leaves to all but invisible scales or discarded them altogether, with the transference of the function of food manufacture from the leaf to the trunk and stems of the plants. These plants grow mostly in the fringes of desert country where the rainfall is sparse and may sometimes fall in great storms all in a few days. Sometimes for months, or even years, on end there may be no rain and the plants are subjected day after day to the scorching rays of a pitiless burning sun with the temperature – as in Death Valley in Arizona—rising to over 55 degrees centigrade.

The problem facing all succulents is to trap and then to hold moisture efficiently. How are they to drink every drop that comes their way in the few short hours that the water is there, and then how are they to store it economically, perhaps through many months of drought, till the next rains come? To collect this moisture has led to many varieties of root action. Some have tuberous roots, especially in very dry areas. Plants such as Euphorbia suzannae, living in stony areas, send their roots deep down into moist areas well below the surface. Others have roots which radiate for yards around so that they can trap even the slightest sinking dew. The next problem is how to store the water economically. Most plants transpire a great deal of water through the pores in their leaves and stems, but succulents have far fewer pores and keep them closed much of the time. Everything is devoted to the necessity of preventing the serious evaporation caused by the prevailing winds and the scorching sun.

Whether the succulent retained or discarded leaves, the plant body tended to become more or less spherical, or at least cylindrical, and the important thing about this approach either to a globe or to a column is that these shapes combine maximum internal tissue potential with minimum surface area. In other words, there is less surface to lose moisture but greater space in which to conserve

it. This process has happened on both sides of the Atlantic. Take a look at the many tall Cerei in the New World. These have evolved their present shapes under similar climatic conditions to the Old World plants such as the vast Candelabra Euphorbias in Africa. The Prickly Pear, as the more commonly known Opuntias are called, have adapted themselves to new conditions more easily than most of the plants and you find them flourishing their pads in many varying climes throughout the world, sometimes as treasures and again as weeds not so many hundred miles apart. Another group of Opuntias, the Cholla, have adapted themselves to even tougher conditions and consist simply of brittle stems, often like signposts.

The reason for the prevalence of spines in cacti is a matter of speculation. It has been suggested that these help to conserve water. They also give some protection, when the plants are young, against the many predatory denizens that roam the deserts during the night, and they afford some additional shade to the plants or act as reflectors to brilliant sunlight. They may assist too in making use of the precious dews which fortunately so often occur in the desert lands.

Spines and thorns occur freely in cactus plants and especially in those of the semi-desert and scrub floras. These prickly outgrowths differ considerably in the manner in which they have arisen and it is important to realize that the thorns of succulent Euphorbias constitute an entirely different structure from the spines so obvious in most cacti, which grow often in clusters out of the areoles.

Curiously enough, where strongly-armed vegetation dominates the landscape, it is often of considerable value to wild animals. After all, there is sometimes nowhere else to go. Foxes of Baja, California burrow under the vicious spines of the 'Creeping Devil' cactus (Machaerocereus) thereby enjoying some shade combined with sound perimeter defences. Ridiculous as it seems, at least one genus of South American birds nests on the very summit of tall column-like cacti. Other birds raise their brood within tunnels in the stems. Lizards see a cactus as a happy hunting ground and have mastered the techniques of camouflage combined with lightning attack. Some of these reptiles even look like cacti. We sympathize with the wild cat who raced to the top of a Cereus cactus in order to get out of the way, and equally so with the unfortunate parachutist who 'fell among thorns' or with the many infantry-men who have hurriedly dived for cover into a hedge of Prickly Pear.

I think that by now you will agree with me that you cannot treat all cactus and succulent plants alike if you are to be successful in their cultivation. You must study their growing habits and the conditions in which they live in their place of origin, and you must try to see how best you can simulate those conditions in the place in which you are growing your own plants. It is all a matter of degree. Fortunately most succulents are tough and they manage to exist under quite adverse circumstances.

Obviously they will do best if properly looked after, but many of them will survive with a period of little or no water, for example, when their owner goes off on holiday. What they will not tolerate is overwatering as this will produce a sodden compost in which they will inevitably rot off and die.

The next problem is how best to sub-divide this vast mass of plants. Usually we do so into two rather loose groups. The ordinary person will say at once 'what on earth is your difficulty? Surely the cacti are the prickly ones and the succulents are the softer looking ones, often in lovely pastel shades?' This description carries us nowhere botanically, and I will cite just two instances to prove the point. Astrophytum myriostigma, which has no spines, is a cactus and Euphorbia grandicornis which is covered with prickles, is not included in the cacti, but is akin to our own wood and meadow spurges. It is instances such as these that make one begin to realize the problems encountered in attempting to classify these groups.

'Cacti' and 'Succulents' is however a well-used method of description which is very useful in catalogues. Botanically, however, it is misleading, as *most cacti are succulents* and *all cacti and succulents are Xerophytes*. 'Cacti and Other Succulents' is another form of nomenclature which is often used, but this implies quite incorrectly that the cacti are numerically far more numerous than the remaining succulent genera. Nevertheless, it is simple and gives the correct impression and is in my opinion the best we have found so far.

Let us now deal with the Cactaceae. The Cactaceae come almost exclusively from the Americas and their geographical distribution affords a fascinating study in itself. America is such a vast continent that throughout its length and breadth you will find almost every type of climatic condition. It is therefore not surprising that many of the cacti come from homes having very diverse climates, with totally different growing conditions. You find them from Canada to the USA and the West Indies, or in Central America, Galapagos and southwards almost to the tip of South America.

The majority come from lands like the sun-scorched plains and prairies of the southern states of the USA and Mexico and the mountains and low grasslands of South America. It is round Arizona and Mexico that most people conjure up visions of the cactus plants of western sagas.

To mention but a few, the huge Saguaro trees and other Cerei, together with many Opuntias, Mammillarias and Echinocereus, come from Arizona, whilst Cephalocereus senilis is a native of Mexico. Some cacti are found in the tropical deserts of Central America and the West Indian islands living always in the glare of the sun, whilst others exist under the shade of trees and shrubs. Plants like Oreocereus and Cleistocactus live on the rocky slopes of the Andes, while the Saguaros and some Cerei, Mammillarias and Opuntias of North America live high up, sometimes under snow, on the lower slopes of Superstition and other mountains. Rebutias and Lobivias come from the hills of Argentina and like cooler conditions, as in their own homes they are often covered by long grass.

Then there is a totally different branch of the cactus family found in both North and South America. These are the vast range of Epiphytic plants which chiefly live in the tropical jungles of Mexico and the eastern coastal regions of South America. They grow in the jungle trees as Epiphytes, in like manner to orchids, living in great humidity in the partial shade afforded by the leaves and branches of the swaying tree tops. They have long waxy stems and branches off which the moisture drops, and they are quite different in shape and structure from other cacti. Despite this utter difference in their look and manner of life, they and their desert brethren all belong to the family Cactaceae.

Some people imagine that Opuntias are indigenous to the Mediterranean basin, Australia and India, but they originally came from America, though now after several centuries of highly successful growth in their new homes they are, like the Agaves, claimed by the inhabitants as native to their country. There is, however, one genus of cacti with representatives in other parts of the world than America and that is Rhipsalis, which is found in Africa, Burma and Ceylon.

From this short account it can be seen that the Cactaceae, with one exception, originated in America, under very varied climatic conditions. There is one important characteristic common to all of them and that is the fact that in every case they live in friable, well-drained soil. No matter whether they come from the arid prairie lands, the snow-covered sides of Superstition Mountain, the rain-soaked jungle forests or the grassland of Argentina, the roots of all of them live in a well-drained soil which is never stagnant. This is a vital point to remember in the cultivation of cacti and one which we must never overlook if we are to grow our plants really well.

All cacti have certain common characteristics. I will not give a botanical description of them, as this may be needlessly complicated. Instead I will try to explain, in less technical language, what these plants look like and what are their chief points.

The great majority of cactus plants, as I have already said, are either long and lanky, often without any branches, or they are spherical, round or flattened out. They often carry long, fearsome-looking spines, sometimes (as in Opuntia tunicata) with a loose sheath over the spine and a kind of fish hook on the end. In some cases these spines are dangerously curved (as in Echinocactus Grusonii) and sometimes they are covered with a mass of minute glochids (stiff, brittle bristles, barbed at the end) as in Opuntia microdasys. Then there are the very tall plants which are mostly in the Cereus group. Most of them have branches and are seen in the background of many Westerns. Do not be dismayed at the thought of these plants in your home! You can buy quite small ones, two or three inches high, for your collection; remember, too, that some of these giant trees may be over 300 years old, which shows that it will take a very long time for your specimens to reach their full height.

All these are what we have been brought up to think of as cacti, and there is usually little difficulty in separating them from other succulents. Once again there are, as always, the exceptions to the rule, and there are some members of the Cactaceae which look more like a fleshy succulent than a normal, tough-looking cactus. One of these is Ariocarpus, often described as resembling a denizen of the sea, with a rosette which seems spineless until you get down to it with a microscope. It often appears half dead—sometimes it is and it may well be sixty or seventy years old. If it comes to you direct from the desert it can be very hard to reroot, as usually its long tap root has either been destroyed on being dug up from its hard native land, or

removed in order to conform with the import regulations of government authorities. Astrophytum myriostigma, 'the Bishop's Cap', is another; it is usually five-sided and smooth without any visible spines, and might easily be confused with the succulent Euphorbia obesa from South Africa. The Pereskias with their small green leaves (a luxury which most cacti have had to forego ages ago) are another exception to the rule.

There is a certain resemblance between some of the tall Candelabra Euphorbias from East Africa and the vast American Cerei. For the beginner, however, I would hasten to add that large cacti normally have three or four or even more spines arising from their areoles, whereas the tall Euphorbias normally only have one or two thorns which are, in fact, technically the ends of the leaves, though they may look very much like spines.

These examples are exceptions rather than the rule and the majority of the other succulents, with their leaves and soft fleshy bodies, do not look the least like any of the Cactaceae. The hundreds of pebble succulents with their tiny fleshy bodies, for instance, could not conceivably be confused with any cactus, nor could the smaller members of the vast Euphorbia family, nor the Crassulas, Sedums or Kalanchoes, to mention but a few of the other succulent plants, which number at least some 4400 species.

Astrophytum, the Star Cactus or Bishop's Cap (from its resemblance to a biretta)

Forest cacti

The Forest Cacti, or Orchid Cacti as they are sometimes called, exist under totally different conditions from the desert plants of America and Africa, for they have always lived in the dense tropical forests of Central and South America under very humid jungle conditions. Millions of years ago there existed in these forests the first true cactus plant, probably resembling the present day Pereskia tribe.

Certain areas changed less than others as the world evolved, and some of the vast forests which survived were those in Central and South America. Elsewhere, most of the cactus family altered their shape and method of life as the temperature and climates changed, but the forest plants, on account of the humid jungle atmosphere in which they lived, did not have to submit to the same radical alterations as their fellow cacti which were compelled to find a means of existence in the scorching sun and bare sandstone rocks of the deserts.

It is probable, however, that in the struggle for survival and Forest Cacti were overshadowed by the branches above them and to seek the sunlight they found it necessary to climb higher into the trees, where their roots could at the same time find pockets of humus in which they could subsist, high up in the crotches of the trees. They are still slightly succulent, as are the orchids which grow alongside them in the jungle trees; like the desert cacti, their water supply is not constant. But they too, by storing water, can survive during dry periods. These Epiphyllanae, which term includes all those Epiphytic cacti closely related to the Epiphyllums, have the following necessary characteristics of a cactus: they are perennial; the seedlings have two or more cotyledons, and they have areoles, on some of which you find the new growth, flowers and spines.

The branches of the Epiphyllums are jointed, with areoles in the sunken crenations of the edges of these stems; the main ones are usually round and woody for the first few inches, after which they become flat or triangular. The Epiphyllums have discarded their true leaves and have a wax-like outer skin which counters evaporation. Like other cacti, they expand when there is plenty of water and contract during a drought, so that a ten-foot cactus plant may only lose an ounce of water a day when a normal tree might lose ten gallons.

The branches may be up to fifteen feet long and up to eight inches wide, though most of them average about three inches. Some of them, during periods of drought, are as thin as paper, whilst others, at times of growth, are anything up to one inch thick at the base. It is interesting that both flat and triangular stems may grow on the same plant, and sometimes a branch starts triangular and then flattens out or vice versa.

These branches or stems function in the same way as leaves and have green cells which, with the assistance of sunlight, transform food into growth and flowers. The roots absorb the water and carry the necessary minerals, when they have been dissolved, to the stems of the plant, where the water is combined with carbon dioxide and converted into sugars and starches for plant growth. During the tropical jungle downpours, the rains are quickly absorbed and the water is stored in the branches and stems, while the root area retains sufficient root moisture to keep the fine roots from drying out. Therefore, they have no need after the rains to spread out or form new roots, as so many of the normal shallow-rooted cacti have to do, and their roots remain confined to a relatively small area.

The plants also have air roots which develop anywhere on the branches. These feed the joints furthest away from the root system and they absorb moisture from the air or from contact with the humus on the branches. For the grower to be able to simulate this way of life and provide a high moisture content in the air, it is important to damp down one's Epiphyllums morning and evening. This serves the dual purpose of supplying the necessary moisture in the atmosphere and keeping the pores of the plant clean.

Pereskia in flower in Dudley Gold's garden in Cuernavaca, Mexico

The plants live in semi-twilight high up in the jungle trees, under the partial shade of the swaying boughs, which also protect them from gales and storms. As the leaves sway and the boughs move to and fro in the wind, so the rays of the sun come and go on the plants below. In this way they get some of the sunlight they require for the development of their necessary foodstuffs, but they remain in sufficient shade to prevent them from drying out and, at the same time, they maintain a high enough degree of humidity. Their roots are anchored to the highly nitrogenous humus lodged in the fissures of the bark of the great trees; and, though short and fine, the roots are strong enough to support these plants, which often hang down through the branches of the trees for ten or fifteen feet towards the ground.

The extreme warmth speeds the evaporation of the soil and in the rainy season drops of water fall incessantly from leaf to leaf. The humidity in the dark, dank atmosphere is over ninety per cent, but, growing as they do high up in the trees well above the sodden ground, their drainage is exceptionally good and the water seeps easily away from the porous humus, leaving their root system nice and damp, but never water-logged. The original Epiphyllums were found in Mexico, though some were subsequently discovered in Central America, on the northern coast of South America, in Amazonia and in Paraguay and other tropical regions of South America.

I have myself seen Epiphytes growing high in the leafy branches of trees, in the forest areas of Central Madagascar and near the northern coast of Jamaica.

European Botanists first discovered these plants in the early part of the nineteenth century, when for the first time they saw their superb pendant white flowers, descending from the great wax-like branches. The blooms of most of the true species are fragrant, and the original sixteen were all white, though there are tinges of yellow, cream and straw-colour on the outer petals of most species. Several of them, like Epiphyllum Cooperi, flower from the base of the plant. The flowers develop slowly at first and it may take up to ten weeks for the buds to open.

In 1812, the English Botanist Haworth (after whom the Haworthia genus was named) coined the name Epiphyllum from the Greek translation of 'upon the leaf'. This refers to the flowers being on what the early writers called the leaf, which we now know as the branch or stem. The name Epiphyllum took the place of Cactus Phyllanthus, which was the name originally given by Linnaeus. In 1819, Haworth discovered a new kind of Epiphyte, which he called Epiphyllum truncatum. In 1831, Link coined the name Phyllocactus (after the Greek word 'Phyllum', a leaf) instead of Epiphyllum, but kept the name Epiphyllum truncatum for Haworth's plant in 1819. This

Epiphytes, including Rhipsalis, pendant high in the trees near the north coast of Jamaica

A group of flowering Epiphyllums

nomenclature held good till 1923, when Britton and Rose affirmed the name Epiphyllum for the sixteen original species which they then accepted. Meanwhile Karl Schumann coined the name Zygocactus, and it still applies to the 'Christmas cactus', Zygocactus truncatus, from the Greek word for 'yoke', in reference to the flower segments which give the appearance of being linked together.

In addition to Epiphyllum, there are several other genera of Epiphyllanae which are closely related to them, including Chiapasis, Nopalxochia, Rhipsalis, Rhipsalidopsis, Schlumbergera and Zygocactus.

The European botanists were thrilled with their discovery of these plants and they brought a few of the original species with their white flowers when they came to Europe. The earliest hybrids recorded were made by Jenkinson and Smith in England in 1830, followed closely by the Germans and later by the French. The original crosses were made with Heliocereus speciosus and Nopalxochia phyllanthoides. In 1840, Epiphyllum crenatum, which flowers on the tips of the stems, was brought to France and was crossed with Heliocereus speciosus. They obtained many new flowers from light yellowish-white and rose shade to orange and deep amber. It was a great step forward. In 1890, Johannes Nicolai in his nursery at Dresden hybridized Schlumbergera, Zygocactus and Rhipsalis and he also introduced 300 new Epiphyllum hybrids. Unfortunately little of his work exists, as all his plants were frozen owing to shortage of coal in World War I. Other great German hybridizers were George Borneman (who produced many German Empress types) and Curt Knebel, who produced many strong types, after he had set himself the task of eliminating many of the attractive though weak hybrids.

About 1930, H. M. Wegener of Los Angeles, California, decided to import Epiphyllum hybrids into America and in a few years he built up a collection of several hundreds. Several other Americans realized how much more could be done to produce new hybrids in the glorious sunshine of California than in the greenhouses of Europe and bit by bit the centre of this hybridization work had shifted back to America, but this time to California. The excellent Epiphyllum Society of America was founded in 1940, and it has established the fact that one of the original homes of these plants was actually along the western coastline of the United States.

Epiphyllums, from top to bottom: Moonlight cream with green centre and marie salmon pink; The pink Samite and Pink Ballet; Deutsche Kaiserin—with small, very attractive pink flowers—lasts particularly well in the house; Kismet with a mauve flower with purple stripes

In their natural habitat

1 North America

As we approached Tucson, we flew across the Sonoran Desert in New Mexico, and from much that we had read we expected to see cactus plants growing in this desert land. All that we saw were miles and miles of rolling sand dunes, with never a sign of a plant, not unlike parts of the Western Desert of Egypt and what one would expect to see in the Sahara or the Gobi Desert.

Another place where we wondered whether we would see cactus plants was around the Grand Canyon, and it was one of the first places we were sent to see. It is indeed one of the Great Wonders of the World but there are no cactus plants up there either. It is far too high – nearly 8000 feet and at the time of our visit, they had just had twenty inches of snow. We arrived at Williams, sixty miles away, at 3 pm, and another heavy snow storm was forecast for that night. We were most anxious to see the Grand Canyon and to get away before darkness fell at about 6 pm, and a good friend told us that the road had been swept of snow and that we could easily get there and back and take photographs of the Canyon in the time available. We were rewarded with an unforgettable sight, as the snow clouds formed up behind the mauve and purple ridges, stretching away beyond the Colorado River which surged along a ravine, a mile below us. We got back safely and spent a pretty cold night in a small motel, while it snowed all night. The next morning we had to buy chains, to ensure a safe passage, but after fifty miles the road cleared and we were able to take off the chains, and by the time we had dropped down a few thousand feet to Phoenix, we ran into warm summer sunshine and blue sky with Bougainvillia and flowering shrubs in all the gardens.

We went on next to our hosts' ranchland round Tucson, and it was here that I was first to realise that the cacti of Arizona grow mostly in grass. Sometimes, as was the case with Agave huascha, in luscious long grass, quite a foot high. During our visit we were sitting writing our letters on chairs outside the ranch house when we heard heavy breathing behind us, and were disconcerted to find a magnificent Hereford bull standing at our backs. This was a pedigree Hereford Ranch and we soon became accustomed to finding ourselves alone with the bulls, who were grazing amongst the cacti in this strange and wonderful land. At over 4000 feet, it was too high for the Saguaros, but on all sides there were Agaves and Yuccas, which looked particularly lovely when the whole countryside changed to orange and gold as the sun set in the evening.

After this first glimpse of the cacti in Arizona, it was interesting to look back on our journey thither across New Mexico. The change between the scattered Creosote plants of the deserts and the first few Chollas is scarcely noticeable. It all takes place in the first few hundred feet, still on the sandy clay of the plain, and as you move up to about 1000 feet you come on to a gravelly-looking surface, which obviously has better drainage. Here you see the first Saguaro and suddenly the scene changes. As you look ahead you see more and more Saguaros in the distance, the Mesquite bushes appear and become closer together as you get higher. There are patches of grass which turn into grassland and pasture as the height increases and you see Prickly Pears, Chollas and Paloverde trees. It is a lovely sight even in the winter, but in the spring, when all the flowers are in bloom, it is glorious and totally unlike the desert land below. We got up to 1500 feet and we found Ocotillos and Barrel Cactus peeping through the longer grass, and as we rose to 3000 feet, Yuccas and Agaves replaced the Saguaros for which the climate was becoming too wet and cold in the lush grassland. As we mounted still further, the evergreen oak appeared, followed by the juniper, which at 7500 feet is joined by the Arizona pine, in country closely resembling Austria and Switzerland. Here the rainfall is twenty inches per year, just double that of the desert.

Now to describe a few of the best-known American cacti. One of the most interesting is the Pereskia, which is the living counterpart of what are believed to have been the original primitive cacti, in the days when they were ordinary plants growing in the tropical forests. They are the only members of the Cactacea who have retained their leaves and branches, and they bloom very profusely with yellow flowers. Then there is the vast Cereus family, one of whose 'big brothers', the Saguaro, grows in great profusion in large stretches of Arizona, and is described later in this chapter. The word Cereus is taken from the Latin word for 'torch', referring to the candelabra-like branches of these tall and elegant plants. About one-sixth of the whole family of Cactaceae consists of the genus Cereus, mostly with names ending in the word 'cereus' but botanical revision has now left comparatively few of the old tall Cereus tribe. Lemaireocereus

Thurberi, named after George Thurber, the botanist member of the Mexican Boundary Commission, is a typical example of this group, known on account of their magnificent shape as the Organ Pipe cacti. They come mostly from the Sonoran Desert in Mexico and Baja, California, and near Ajo in southern Arizona many of these trees are preserved in what is known as The Organ Cactus National Monument. They have yellow-green stems which, unlike those of the Saguaro, originate at the base of the tree and form vast clusters of arms, often eight inches in diameter which stretch upwards from ground level to a height of some fifteen feet in Arizona, rising to twenty-five to thirty feet further south in Mexico.

This magnificent plant has a pale greenish-white flower about one and a half inches in diameter, which blooms near the tops of the branches in May and June. Its egg-shaped red fruit is much prized by the Indians, as it has a very high sugar content, and the Mexicans call the plant Pitahaya dulce, 'The Sweet Fruit'—a tribute both to the toughness of its spine and the sweetness of its fruit. It is susceptible to frost and so you do not find it growing alongside the Saguaro in the higher mountain slopes. However, even if the tip of a growing branch is severely damaged by frost, the branch itself will continue to live and to swell in girth to its normal dimensions. In cultivation they are certainly not so hardy as the other Cerei. The Organ Pipe National Monument is well worth a visit. It borders on Mexico and you have the interest of driving along a good gravel road beside the frontier. Some of the stands of Lemaireocereus Thurberi are very fine, and close by there is a most interesting group of Lophocereus Schottii, often called senita, due to the hairy tops of the stems when the plants are flowering.

There are said to be nearly 450 kinds of night-blooming cacti, which include many Cereus. They nearly all have white flowers, sometimes faintly tinged with other colours. Many have a heavy scent which guides the insects to them during the night. Even the bees come to them during the hour or so before dawn, and again in the evening just before the petals close. You find them in the southern extremes of the United States and in Central and South America. In Hawaii too, there is Hylocereus undatus known as 'The Wavy Forest Cereus', which makes a lovely scented hedge, especially when the flowers are in bloom on a warm night. It is a native of the West Indies and was probably taken from there to Hawaii for use as a garden hedge.

Another night-flowerer is Peniocereus Greggii, 'Queen of The Night', with its long, thin stick-like stems studded with groups of some ten to twelve tiny black spines. Beneath the shallow roots system there is a long tuber, sometimes weighing up to eighty pounds, which grows very deep like a tap root and makes the plant very difficult to dig up

without damage. This tuber functions as the storage place for food and water during droughts, and when the tender stems above ground are broken, new ones shoot up from the tuber. It is an ugly-looking plant which usually grows under other larger bushes for protection and support, but all this is forgotten when the loveliness of its flower and the perfection of its scent come into their own on the

Sunset on Lemaireocereus Thurberi, the 'organ pipe Cactus'

nights when it bursts into flower. Soon after sunset you can literally watch the petals begin to open, until they finally reach as much as six inches in diameter. The inner petals are creamy-white and the sepals may be lavender, green or purple. On a warm night, you may have thirty blooms open at once, and sometimes, on very hot nights, most of the plants in one area will bloom together, as the very high temperatures force the undeveloped buds to open at the same time as the mature ones. They last only one night but the sight of the flowers and their scent in that part of the forest on that particular night are an experience beyond belief.

Some of the largest flowers are found among the Moon Cerei (Selenicereus) a group of plants with stems that climb and trail like vines, often twenty feet in length. Selenicereus grandiflorus from the West Indies, known as 'The King Of The Night', is the best known of them with a most fragrant flower, often ten inches in diameter. Another plant also known as 'Queen Of The Night' produces the largest flower of all – thirteen inches in diameter, with the usual white petals and golden sepals. Another night-blooming cactus is Wilcoxia, with its root system of small tubers, which is mostly found in the Sonoran Desert. Its thin stems are sometimes five feet long and they are difficult to see as they thread their way through the branches of trees and bush.

Another large group of heavily-spined plants are the Barrel Cacti, which include the genus Ferocactus. They usually lean in the general direction of the sun and have consequently earned for themselves the name of 'Compass Cacti'. They are thick, massive plants, but seldom very tall; though I have seen, near Tucson, one magnificent specimen of Ferocactus Wislezenii over nine feet high. They differ from the Hedgehog Cactus in that the flowers bloom on the extreme top of the plant, where they often emerge from a dense pad of hairs. Curiously enough, the larger plants have smaller flowers than their smaller brethren, and they have the toughest, longest and broadest spines of all cacti. Some of the plants eventually become cylindrical with a diameter of around two feet. The flowers, which bloom from June to September, are two to three inches across, grow in circular clusters, and vary in colour from yellow and orange to dark red. In winter, the plants are crowned with bright yellow fruit sometimes looking like pineapples, though considerably smaller and filled with black seeds which the birds often eat. The plant is known as the Candy Cactus from the fact that the white tissue of the plant can be cut into small cubes, which are boiled in clear water to remove the bitterness. After a final boil in hot syrup of pinche (the Mexican brown sugar), each piece is rolled in bar sugar and glazed in the sun.

During the rainy season the bigger plants often become water-logged and fall over but even so they continue to live and flower while flat on the ground.

A vast Ferocactus Wislezenii leaning towards the sun at Tucson

Ferocactus acanthoides with its lovely red spines nestling in the rocks

Their growth is very slow, and the giant Barrel Cactus, although only nine feet in height with similar girth and weighing several thousand pounds, may well be 500 or 600 years old. Then we have several species which are the dream and envy of many an experienced collector. The Ariocarpus, or 'Living Rock,' is one of them with its inert-looking, close rosette of pointed tubercles. There are too, the Lophophoras or Anhaloniums, known as the Mescal Button or Peyote, which are devoid of spines and look somewhat like a denizen of the sea. They were used by the Indians to give them religious hallucinations, since they contain an alkaloid from which the drug Mescalin is made. There are many interesting Astrophytums including Astrophytum myriostigma, The Bishop's Cap, and Leuchtenbergia principis, the Agave Cactus, which consists of a stout root surmounted by a cluster of triangular projections, each topped by a cluster of spines with large and fragrant flowers.

Another well-known group is that known as the Hedgehog Cacti, which is the name given to the genus Echinocereus. This name is derived from the Greek word echines meaning a hedgehog and the Latin word cereus, 'a torch'. It is one of the most beautiful flowering cacti and is often known as the Strawberry Cactus, as some of them bear fruit with a taste like that of strawberries. The plants are low and column-like, with a group of stems up to fifteen inches high. A clump of Echinocereus Engelmannii when it flowers in April and May is a sight to behold, with its clusters of purplish-pink flowers. One plant at the University of Arizona had several hundred blooms open at one time.

The crimson Echinocereus triglochidiatus from New Mexico can also be a magnificent sight, sometimes flowering in moulds of a hundred stems or more, as wide as four feet and a foot high, often with over fifty claret or crimson blooms on one plant. These plants are not big, and during much of the year they appear insignificant but when they do bloom they produce the most vivid colours and are very much in demand for planting out in cactus gardens in Arizona.

Echinocereus in Phoenix Botanical Gardens

A lovely Echinocereus with purple flowers with a yellow centre and a Rainbow Cactus

Echinocereus triglochidiatus and the Rainbow Cactus amid the rocks

Echinocereus pectinatus, the Rainbow Cactus, is a particularly lovely plant. When it blooms it has clusters of glorious pink flowers, and during the rest of the year, particularly if it is growing in full sunlight, it has merging stripes of mauve to pink colouring around its body. It is chiefly found in Mexico, but when I was in Arizona I saw many fine plants, mostly growing in grassland.

The Mammillarias or Pincushion and Fishhook Cacti are another most interesting tribe. They are small plants, many of which flourish under the shade of larger plants and bushes. Amongst the group you find Mammillarias, Neobesseyas, Escobarias and Neolloydias. The flowers usually bloom in a ring round the side of the plant and each year the new flowers appear above the ring of the old ones, often above last year's seedpods. A large number of these plants also come from Mexico and some from Venezuela. In this group there are also the 'Top-Flowering Cacti', the Coryphanthas, one of which, Coryphantha vivipara, is also found

in Manitoba in Canada. They are sometimes known as 'Rising Biscuits', as their stems usually flatten out in winter from dehydration. After the rains they bear lavender and pink flowers and then, as their nickname suggests, they swell into a mould of small globes.

The Yuccas are another interesting group, of which over thirty species are found in the United States. They vary greatly in size and shape and the best-known is the Joshua tree, Yucca brevifolia, which is the tallest and looks most like a tree. A visit to the Joshua Tree National Monument, a few miles from Palm Springs, California, is well worth while. There are many impressive, very old and tall Joshua trees growing in magnificent scenery, often with a background of vast, perilously-perched rocks.

Most Yuccas have rosettes of sharp-pointed leaves. They grow chiefly on the higher ground over 4000 feet, where, in the higher rainfall and better soil, they make large plants, sometimes with fifteen-foot flower spikes, like those of the coastal

A striking group of Echinocereus pectinatus (top) and a lovely specimen (below)

A fine group of well-coloured Rainbow Cactus

regions. You also find them closer to the desert regions, but there they are smaller and more stunted in their growth. They are plants of the Lily family but, like cacti, they are drought-resistant, and so we find them growing happily alongside our other succulent plants, though they are not strictly succulents. The flowers are lightly clustered along an erect flower stalk, though the individual blossoms are often pendant. They open at night, but do not close during the day as so often happens with the night-flowering plants.

Some Mesembryanthemums have become so well naturalized as to merit inclusion in the floras, notably Carpobrotus on the California coasts, and Cryophytum crystallimum which, incidentally, is liable to turn up almost anywhere in the world. The Agaves, which include the Sisal plant, are widely naturalized and have become endemic to many parts of the world. Over 300 species, however, are recognised as native to the USA, the West Indies and Tropical America.

The United States is very rich in botanical and desert gardens and possesses in its Universities and Botanical Societies many expert botanists who are most knowledgeable on the subject of Xerophytic plants. At Tucson, there is a most interesting desert garden at the Arizona Sonoran Desert Museum, with it is a delightful zoological collection of desert animals, of which the smaller ones are most attractively exhibited under the most natural conditions behind glass windows with natural trees and grasses as part of most intriguing dioramas. At Phoenix, too, there is the Desert Botanical Garden of Arizona, with an excellent variety of cacti in outside beds and also in a large slatted shade house. Further west, in California, there is the fascinating cactus garden at the Huntington Library at San Marino near Los Angeles which contains succulent plants from the world over. Further north, at the University of California at Berkeley, near San Francisco, there is another wonderful cactus garden in which those plants from North America,

A magnificent Joshua tree amid the rocks near Palm Springs

Mexico, South America and Africa that will stand up to the coastal climate of California are laid out in such a way that the plants of each country can be studied by themselves in separate beds. There is also a wonderful collection of 4000 specimens, including many very rare genera, in a large greenhouse.

Even in a large volume it would be impossible to adequately describe all the Xerophytic succulent plants of America or the country-side in which they live, so I have confined myself to this limited survey, but on the next few pages I am going to deal in somewhat greater detail with the Saguaros and the Opuntias.

Saguaro Land

I held my breath, as far away in the distance I saw my first Saguaro—officially known as Carnegiea gigantea but commonly known in Arizona as 'Old Saguaro', or the Giant Cactus. In that thrilling moment I realised that at long last I had seen my first 'Sage of the Desert' whose age may well have been over 200 years. As I went on, there were Saguaros around me on all sides, stretching far into the distance towards the mountains, where even on the slopes of the Superstition Mountains they were clinging precariously to the cliffs.

The Saguaro is mostly to be found in Arizona and Baja California, and there is to my mind no doubt that it is the most majestic and inspiring of all cacti. Each one of them stands like a huge sentinel, often thirty to fifty feet tall—alone in its glory—yet it is in actual fact just one of a vast assembly of succulent giants. Its great arms radiate from the trunk well above ground level in a fan-shaped group, usually pointing towards heaven and yet sometimes twisted in the most fantastic shapes, starting vertically and finishing horizontally and even, for no apparent reason, once again dipping downwards.

The author by a Saguaro showing the typically fantastic shapes of the branches

A large Saguaro with its branches entwined in fantastic shapes

**A giant Echinocactus Grusonii in the
Huntington Gardens in California—over
one hundred years old**

Unlike many other succulent plants, it has only a comparatively short tap root and relies on long, shallow-growing lateral roots, sometimes twenty or thirty feet in length, which force their way outwards in all directions in such a manner as to enable it to collect as much as possible of the precious water when the rains come. The Saguaros are jealous of any intruder into their own particular water zone and you very seldom see a young cactus growing within the area covered by the roots of an older plant; their roots suck up so much of the available water that there is practically none left to share.

The trunks are thick and massive and heavily pleated like an accordion, while the branches are also pleated to retain moisture. Their outer hide is tough enough to withstand the wind and sunshine, which might otherwise rob them of the water they so carefully store. The white hulk within their pleats is a reservoir of stored-up water, and if cut with a knife it is quite soft, like the rind of a ripe melon. The average rainfall in the Saguaro areas is between five and seventeen inches a year, and after the rains the plants often increase their girth by an inch or more. The tremendous weight of the plant, sometimes up to ten or fifteen tons, is supported by very strong cylindrical cores of several dozen rods up to two inches in diameter. This heavy weight produces a difficult anchorage problem, for in the Saguaro forests there are very strong winds, and sometimes in the rainy weather when the ground is soft, the root anchorage is not tough enough to support several tons of giant cactus swaying in the wind. In one part of the Sonoran Desert, many of the Saguaros have in fact been blown over and are lying half-buried in the sand, all pointing in the same

A fine Saguaro cristate in the Desert Museum at Tucson

The late Lady Leese by the tallest Saguaro—58 feet high—in the Tucson National Park

direction. Uprooted like this they can still live for long periods in the dry atmosphere of the desert, taking several years to die.

Their growth is very slow and one young specimen in Arizona took thirty-nine years to grow thirty-one inches. They average half an inch a year during the first thirty years. If they grow as slowly as that in the glorious sunshine in Arizona, is it any wonder that they do so exceptionally slowly in Europe? As young plants, they are very narrow at the base of their stems, gradually widening out as they grow taller, almost like a Barrel Cactus. I have a plant like this at Worfield that is some two-and-a-half feet high and yet must be over thirty years old. For the first sixty or seventy years of their life the spines are a heavy reddish colour, turning black and, as they mature to a flowering age, yellow. When one is looking at these huge trees, one often wonders about the real reason for their great spines. At the base of the trunk they undoubtedly give protection against animals, and they certainly provide some shade to the plants themselves against day after day of unbroken sunshine. At the ends of the bloom-bearing branches the areoles are heavily felted. Most of the plant's epidermis, however, is free from felt and quite bare, except for the spine clusters that are spaced in rows on top of each rib. Curiously enough, the old areoles do not have felt.

There are dozens of cavities in the trunks, made and used by birds, rats and snakes as nests and sleeping quarters; while spiders, silver-fish and larvae live in the crotches of the branches. They are all amply protected against marauders by the terrific spines.

An Elf Owl on its nest in a Saguaro

After the spring rains in April or May, the Saguaro produces buds some five inches long which open very quickly with clusters of white or greenish-white wax-like petals, while the myriads of yellow stamens on the flower's throat look like fur. The flowers have an incredible number of stamens: over 3000 were once counted in one blossom. The flowers open in the late evening and usually close during the following morning, but if the weather is cool and cloudy they may remain open till the afternoon.

The 'Red Flowers,' as the fruit is sometimes called, have a red pulp of high sugar content, with a slightly acid flavour, which is eaten by the white-wing dove, the elf owl and many other birds. The fruit, which is about three inches long and half as thick, ripens in June or July, when it splits into two or more pieces, which curl back and reveal a red pulp with small black seeds. The seeds are rich in fats and at one time were used for chicken feed.

In the summer of each year, the Papago Indians gather the Saguaro fruit. Each family goes to their own reserved area where they pitch a camp. They use the traditional stick of their tribe, anything between fifteen and forty feet long with a cross piece to pick off the fruit. The women pick the ripe fruit when it is red and has burst open. The meaty centre part is eaten during the camp and the juice is drained off and used as a drink. The pulp is boiled down and stored in pottery jars with tops and sealed down with clay, for use as dried fruit and jam when they get home. Much of the seed is used as feed for chickens and pigs, and sometimes the first fruits are used for ceremonial religious drinking vessels. The birds carry away many of the seeds to the Paloverde trees in which they roost. But the majority of seeds fall off the trees on to the leaf-mould underneath, where they are protected by the undergrowth while they await the summer rains to start off their germination.

If you are fortunate enough to go to Tucson, you will find two particularly interesting and prolific colonies of Saguaros. The best known is the Saguaro National Monument, an area of 53,000 acres a few miles from the city. Here are many of the tallest and oldest known Saguaro—some may even be four or five hundred years old. At first sight you will think these are magnificent specimens of trees, fine and healthy, but if you look into them carefully you will find them gnarled with old age and often riddled with the holes made by birds and rodents for their nests and resting places.

Here and there you will find gaunt skeletons of rod-like wooden bones standing bleakly above heaps of brittle, crumpled débris of what were once healthy, fleshy arms. As you look further, you see the beautiful green bodies of some of these giants fading into masses of black, fetid slime, which slides to the ground to become a loathsome mess infected with maggots and other insects.

The trouble seems worse where the Saguaros are

close together and the infection can therefore spread more easily; and it is particularly bad in the National Monument. The University of Arizona is working very hard on this problem—and their challenge is a great one. For if they fail, this giant cactus forest may well disappear. Scientists believe that the disease is carried in the intestines of a tiny caterpillar called Cactobrosis Fernaldalis. The larva lives in the soft plant tissue, eating tunnels at random, in which the infection soon appears. The experts hope that the work has progressed enough to kill the moth, but it is difficult to see how any plan to eliminate the eggs can be applied to those vast forest areas on the slopes of the mountains; and surely if disease grips these strongholds, widespread infection could all too easily sweep down again to the masses of trees on the plain below.

Some very interesting experiments have been carried out at the University of Arizona on the germination of the Saguaro, and there is little doubt that the seeds will not germinate unless they have a warm enough temperature, together with sufficient humidity. They must not have too great heat when they are young seedlings, yet they must have sufficient light intensity. You would imagine that the whole ground round these giants would be full of young seedlings, but even under the most favourable conditions only a fraction of the seeds germinate and still fewer reach maturity. For the sheep and cattle trample down the undergrowth and then there is no protection for the young plants against the fierce, unbroken midday sun. Furthermore, the desert rodents eat many of the seedlings that do survive. Possibly the settlers are also to blame, for they have waged a relentless war against the coyotes, which had hitherto kept the rodents in check. At any rate, whatever the real cause, young Saguaro trees, though outwardly numerous, are few in proportion to the myriad of seeds produced.

As a result of this shortage of young plants, it looks as if in a hundred years' time there may be very few Saguaros left in the National Monument, but luckily there is, a short distance away, another great colony of Saguaros, a few miles beyond the wonderful Desert Museum. These Saguaros are much younger and consequently not nearly so tall as those in the Saguaro National Park, but they are equally majestic as they are so intensely green and healthy. Here is one area where there is the greatest known concentration of Saguaros in the world.

You have only to move a few hundred feet higher or lower than the elevation round the Desert Museum and you find few, if any, Saguaros. If you drop down below one thousand feet into the plain round Tucson you will find a sandy clay, not pervious to water and holding little vegetation except the Creosote bush or a low Mesquite tree. It is quite unlike Saguaro land with its gravelly surface and excellent drainage, where the rain soaks in comparatively easily, so that the long-spreading roots of the Saguaros can absorb the maximum moisture. If at the other end of the scale you go higher than 4500 feet, you again notice that the Saguaros begin to thin out. At the start you find Ocotillos and then, as you go higher, Yuccas and Agaves. After a while they grow among junipers and higher up the hillsides among pines and scrub oaks. Here, as on the Californian coast, it is too wet for the Saguaros. They will rot off and in the colder weather they are too full of moisture to stand up to the frosts which you sometimes get on these heights.

Saguaroland is indeed a fascinating place for the plant lover and it has recently, also become a popular resort for those wishing to avoid the rigours of a cold winter. It was the search for a better climate that drew Herb Wood to Tucson after he had had a bad fall from high scaffolding and was told by the doctor, one awful morning, that he would never walk again. He had a wife and five small children. He remembered the climate of Arizona which he had visited some years before, and he felt that if he could get back to the warm, dry air of Tucson he might perhaps have a chance to walk again. By sheer guts and with the help of friends he learned in a few months to walk without crutches and he decided to send for his family. He had acquired a plot of land eight miles from Tucson, and the next thing to be done was to build a house on it. Timber required money and he had none. He remembered how in his early wanderings he had seen the Papago and Pima Indians using dead Saguaro ribs in the construction of their dwellings. There were plenty of rocks with which to build the walls of his house, and he used the ribs of the dead trees for his rafters and support poles. By this means a house was built. Furniture was his next problem and once more the dead Saguaro and the Jumping Cholla solved the problem. Soon the whole house was furnished and his friends were so appreciative of his work that he felt that there was an opportunity for him to make money by selling furniture. He gathered the ribs from dead Saguaro and Jumping Chollas in the desert and seasoned them round the house. Soon he was selling the furniture to passersby and visitors as quickly as he could make it. The Saguaro ribs were used for the tables, chairs and cupboards and the Cholla proved admirable for lamp standards, bookends and the smaller pieces of furniture. The wood retains its natural appearance, and this attribute has been the basis of the success of Herb Wood's business, for which only a few tools are necessary.

It is to be hoped that these great Saguaro Forests will never be allowed to disappear. If this were to happen it would be a tragedy no less saddening than would be the extermination of the giant Redwood trees of the Pacific Coast. For when a visitor gazes at the largest of the hundreds of known species of cacti, native only to the western hemisphere, he is looking at something typically and totally American.

The Opuntias

The Opuntia is one of the best known cacti in the world, commonly described by most people as the Prickly Pear. Yet there are few who realize that the country of origin of the whole genus is America and still fewer who know that, quite apart from the well-known Prickly Pears with their large pads, there are also in America alone at least twenty of the Cholla type.

We will deal now with the Prickly Pear, which is supposed to have been in existence for fifty million years. It is known that fossil collectors have found this oldest of all known cacti plainly imprinted on a split piece of eocene shale in the Green Valley of Utah. Its oval, flattened joints resemble the Prickly Pear of today, but this 'Dawn Cactus,' as it was first called, must have been thriving in a very different climate. For fossil leaves and twigs of other plants found in the same area prove that the climate was then warm and humid, possibly much like the forests in which the original Epiphyllum or Orchid Cactus first lived. As the climate changed, other species gave up the struggle but the tough Prickly Pear lived on, and doubtless it will survive for another fifty million years, insulated as it is against a changing climate. There are over three hundred species, and it is believed to have originated in Mexico. It can now be found in nearly every state in the USA, as far south as the Straits of Magellan, in Australia, in India, in Africa and in many parts of southern Europe. To gain this astonishing foothold in every kind of climate, it has developed different peculiarities in each place.

Some have spines as insulation against the heat or cold, some are spineless with tough leathery hides. Others have a dense covering of white hairs which gives them shade from the intense heat and at the same time helps them to conserve moisture. In the hot regions they are large and tree-like, whilst in colder regions they are represented by tiny ground creepers. In the colder climes, when winter sets in, they dehydrate their pads in order to prevent freezing, and in deserts they can hold water through long periods of unbroken drought. Their flowers are mostly yellow, though in the intense heat of the desert sun, they may turn burnt-orange, brown or red. The blooms last a day only in great heat, though on a detached pad they will live for two or three days, and in cool spring weather they may last up to two or even five days. The flowers are very striking, and a bank of Opuntias in full bloom can be a wonderful sight. Although it is the oldest of all cacti, the period of life of any particular Opuntia is often not more than twenty years, but to make up for this short lifetime, its power of propagation, both vegetatively and by seed, is very quick. When a plant is getting towards the end of its life, the joints break off, some rot, but most of them fall to the ground where they form roots and start to grow. By this means they not only keep pace in the reproduction of their species, but they multiply prolifically, as they have done in countries like Australia, South Africa and India where they have taken complete control of the countryside and are now regarded as pests. They have, in fact, owing to their easy propagation during the last few hundred

The tongue-shaped Opuntia linguiformis

years, travelled all over the world, and in many countries along the Mediterranean coast they have become a characteristic feature of the landscape—so much so that most people imagine they are indigenous to these countries.

They have become very strong growers and their power of resistance is incredible. In the very hard winter of 1956 on the Costa Brava in Spain, they had night after night of continuous heavy frost. All the older Opuntias, often up to twelve and fifteen feet high, were seemingly killed. Their branches fell off and the trunks remained like gaunt brown skeletons standing vertical from the ground. When I went there the following September, the whole ground round these plants looked as if it had been planted out with little green Opuntia pads growing away strongly to perpetuate the life of their species.

Let us now look at some of the better-known Arizona Opuntias. Opuntia Engelmannii, called after Dr Engelmann who wrote some of the earliest books on the American cacti, is one of the most widely distributed of the Arizona Prickly Pears. They are found in the foothills between 1200 and 4500 feet up, where they grow in large clumps, often several feet across, alongside the Paloverdes and Saguaros. When they are in full bloom in April and May, with their large satiny-yellow flowers, often three inches across, they seem to catch and reflect the sun so that on a bright day in May these great splashes of colour are a glorious sight. At fruiting time, too, they are a lovely spectacle with their reddish-purple fruit showing in rows along the upper sides of the pads. Then there is Opuntia basilaris, the Beavertail Cactus, which is difficult to cultivate from seed, with its rather smaller and extremely attractive purple flower. The Beavertails do best in a sandy soil and are found up to 3000 feet, where they flower between April and June according to their altitude. The purplish pads are most attractive, especially if they are heart-shaped. They are studded with little groups of small barbed hairs which get caught up in one's hand very easily. The tiny raised spots on the pads replace the more obvious large spines on other species of Opuntia, but each of these contains a large number of innocent-looking but thoroughly barbed hairs called clochids. If you get these all over your clothing you are in for quite a party with them.

Then there is the spineless Prickly Pear, Opuntia lævis, with a sprawling, rather bushy habit, some two to six feet high and several feet in diameter. It has pale grey or white spines, which are sometimes reddish at the extreme bases. It has a light yellow flower about two-and-a-half inches long with a non-spiny reddish fruit. Its spineless character makes it a favourite food for animals and in many places cattle have exterminated the species. It is also eaten by woodrats and other rodents, so you only find it now on inaccessible ledges and canyons in the mountains, mostly in the upper parts of the

desert. Luther Burbank also experimented with some success in the development of the spineless Prickly Pear for livestock food, but his trial plants were at once eaten by rodents and other marauding animals.

The Prickly Pear can however be planted up commercially as a sound financial crop, as was done on a farm of some twenty-eight acres north-west of Lakeside near San Diego, California, belonging to the Maniscalo family, who came over to America from Sicily. Hundreds of giant Opuntias stand here in long rows, where they are fertilized, irrigated and sprayed like any other crop. When the fruit has set, the buds are disbudded by hand, after which each pear is de-spined by the workers who go along the plants, brushing them with a broom of slender tree boughs tied to the end of an eight-foot pole.

Between mid-August and October, when the crop is ripe, men wearing heavy canvas clothing and leather gauntlets cut off the fruit—some working from ground level, others leaning from eight-foot three-legged ladders.

The fruit is then taken to the packing shed, where the pears are passed through a machine with roller brushes to take off any spines that are left, and girls wrap them in paper and pack them in boxes, of which a refrigerator car will take 1800. The whole crop, usually consisting of about fifteen cars a year, is sent off on the nine-day journey to New York and other centres where the Prickly Pear is considered a great delicacy, especially by people from Mediterranean and Latin-American countries.

The Prickly Pear makes a formidable hedge. One of the oldest hedges is round the San Diego Mission, where the original hedge is as strong as ever, though all the buildings have been restored. Another fine hedge was planted at Los Coches Creek near El Cajon in 1859. It consists of three varieties of Prickly Pear, each chosen for the sweetness of its fruit. It stands strongly today, seventy feet wide and over all these years its barbs have successfully kept out cattle, horses and wild hogs (coches) after which the creek was named and which were a menace to the inhabitants.

Opuntia versicolor in flower

A Prickly Pear farm with Opuntias grown for fruit

Opuntia Basilaris with its lovely mauve leaves and pink flower

We will now move on to the Cholla branch of the Opuntias, which have cylindrical joints as opposed to the flat-jointed Prickly Pear. The name Cholla is Spanish, meaning head-shaped, since the crown, formed by the branches and joints, is sometimes shaped like a human head. In Arizona you find some twenty species of Chollas. The tree grows up to twelve feet or more in height, sometimes tall and branched, sometimes compact and spreading. The branches are round and have joints that are linked like sausages and which vary in size from thin pencil-shaped tapers on the small plants to large stems almost like stags' antlers on the larger ones. The joints of some species are densely covered with glittering gold and silver spines, which are a snare and delusion as they are very definitely a form of beauty to be admired from a respectful distance. The joints have the habit of falling off, often at the slightest touch or vibration, and you find the ground under the trees littered with joints, sometimes several inches long, with small barbs of spines on a green background, a most unnecessarily vicious piece of work. The joints drop most noticeably during long periods of drought, perhaps to enable the plant to conserve moisture better by shedding any part of it that might draw away water and partly, perhaps, to ensure future propagation of the species by rooting, in case the parent plant should not survive the drought. Some of the joints root quickly where they fall and grow into new plants, others are trampled by cattle and other animals, which in their turn carry the broken joints on their feet to new places where they fall or are brushed off on the ground to become the forerunners of yet another colony of Chollas. Joints that have dropped but not yet rooted are almost like a living object

27

from the animal world in their ability to cling to your shoes or socks and stick their spines into you. Some of these spines have loose-fitting sheaths with a barb on the end, as in Opuntia tunicata. You can be in real difficulty with them, as the harder you pull, the wider the little barbs open and the more it hurts, until with a spurt of blood the spine eventually comes free. If you get one in your shoe or ankle, it is wise to think first before you grip it with your hand and try to pull it out—otherwise you may quite easily find that hand, ankle and shoe are all stuck very painfully together. The pain soon passes and you feel no ill effects, though it is a good precaution to put a little iodine on the place.

The pack rats and sometimes the squirrels use these spiny 'nobbins,' as they are known in America, to fence every avenue leading to their nests and also those leading them to their usual feeding ground. These clean animals have their lavatories outside their nests and the pathways to them are easy to see, as they are swept clean and tidy and are surrounded by these spiky walls. The spines are sharp enough to pierce the hide of any animal, and yet the pack rats, with their gentle, soft mouths, handle these nobbins with great ease and no apparent harm to themselves.

There are several types of Chollas, and on one day out in the desert round Tucson in Arizona, I was lucky enough to see a good specimen of some of the best-known types—the Staghorn, the Cane, the Chain and the Jumping Chollas. To start with, there was Opuntia versicolor, which is a typical Staghorn or tree Cholla and is found at 2000 to 3000 feet in

Southern Arizona and Northern Mexico—usually in arroyo bottoms or well-watered higher levels. It has a definite trunk, seldom as high as twelve feet with distinctive, intricately-branched stems of a purple or reddish colour. The flowers are very beautiful, varying from yellow and orange to bronze and red. The mature fruit is green and tinged with purple and red. Nearby was the Cane Cholla, Opuntia spinosior, usually three to eight feet high, a shrubby plant which is not unlike Opuntia imbricata. It has branches in whorls which spread at right angles. The flowers range from white to yellow, purple or red and the fruit when mature is lemon-yellow and persists through the following winter. It is common in Arizona in the higher grasslands at 2000 to 7000 feet. Quite close to these two we found the Chain Fruit Cholla, Opuntia fulgida, known sometimes as the Jumping Cholla. It also is tree-like three to fifteen feet high, and seems to be weeping in habit, because of the long chain of old fruit, by means of which you can assess the age of the plant. The spines are straw-coloured and the flowers are pink or white with lavender streaks. The fruit is green and persists often for many years, frequently bearing flowers and fruit on the fruit of last year, until long chains are formed. They range over a large area between 1000 and 4500 feet in Arizona and Mexico, and in some areas round Tucson they are to be found in dense groves with their black trunks and candelabra-like branches.

Near the village of Sells, on my way to the Organ Pipe National Monument, I was shown a whole hillside of Opuntia bigelovii, the Teddy Bear Cholla —a veritable 'field of the cloth of gold' gleaming in the sunlight. It took one's breath away, but one soon had to come back to earth, as nobbins lay everywhere on the ground, and a careless move would fix one of them relentlessly to shoe or ankle. They are columnar Chollas with a main trunk, black on the lower part, two to five feet high. The barbed spines are straw-coloured. The flowers are yellow or white, streaked with lavender, and the fruit is green. Propagation is usually vegetative by means of the joints which fall on the ground. They are usually to be found on hot rocky hill sides facing south, at anything up to 3000 feet in Arizona and Mexico.

There is also the Buckthorn Cholla, Opuntia acanthocarpa, sometimes a shrub of four or six feet high, but often with a sprawling habit. Its individual branches are long and resemble the antlers of a deer. The spines are straw-coloured and the flowers are usually red or yellow.

There are those who say that the treasure trove of the cactaceae lies in Mexico, where there are to be found the greatest variety and many of the most interesting genera in country that is still largely unspoiled. Many of the plants are difficult of access, they still live in comparative scarcity and propagate unhindered and I shall describe what I saw for myself in Mexico in the next section.

The golden Teddy Bear Cholla Cactus near Sells in Arizona

In their natural habitat

2 Mexico

We flew into Mexico City across a cultivated plateau –over 7000 feet high and dominated always by two great snow-covered volcanoes. The centre of Mexico City is very fine, and its avenues, statues and world-famous fountains remind one of the spacious planning of the Place de la Concorde in Paris. Like Egypt or India, Mexico is a country of great and varied extremes. In the back streets of Mexico City you find great poverty, and in the villages most people live in huts, often built with the wood of Cholla and Ocotillo. In Mexico City you see numbers of fine American cars, but you see few automobiles on the country roads, where the villages are served by a large number of buses–some large and expensive, and many rickety-looking local ones. The population is very mixed: there is a little Spanish and American blood, but it is mostly Indian. You can still see some interesting temples of the earlier native civilizations which must have been cultured, educated and comparatively peaceful, until they were swept away by the fierce Aztec rulers, who in turn fell to Cortez and his Spaniards, bringing with them the Catholic religion and the civilization of Spain.

In the countryside today it is the Indian characteristics which survive in the agriculture and life in the villages, though in even the smallest towns there are typical Spanish houses, with lovely patios and grilled doors, behind uncompromising blank walls. We hired a car in Mexico City and motored off in a southerly direction through the city of Puebla to Tehuacan, situated some 200 miles away in a barren, sandy, undulating area where we were to find our first spectacle of Mexican Cacti. We made our first stop north of Tehuacan and here we saw, on a hillside near the road, what appeared to be a wood of fir trees, but when we got closer, it turned out to be a vast collection of tall, bushed Cereus chichipe. In the village below, we had our first sight of the cactus hedges which we were to find in many villages, in this case the green stems of Lemaireocereus spachianus, with its lovely scented, large white flowers. Outside the village, nestling between two stones, was a perfect specimen of the tiny white Solisia pectinata, but it was not till we had passed through Tehuacan that we came on the land of our dreams. We climbed up a small escarpment and suddenly found ourselves surrounded on both sides of the road by tall white Lemaireocereus holyanus, with large Barrel Ferocactus grandis lying amongst them. We went over the next crest

and the view suddenly changed to the equally tall grey Cephalocereus Hoppenstedtii, which were particularly interesting, with the tops of all the stems pointing towards the north. Amongst them were growing some branched green Myrtillocactus Schenkii, with their small white flowers along their branches.

A mile or so further on, the whole picture changed again, and we were driving amid a set of quite new plants. This time it was a veritable forest of tall green trees–Cephalocereus tetetzo, growing so close together that they almost appeared to be touching one another. Then the road descended a thousand feet or so, and we found a new tree–the branched and white-tipped Cephalocereus chrysacanta–growing in a countryside covered with thickets and bushes, with Acacias in bloom with their yellow flowers and golden Hechtias, Wilcoxia viperina and Mammillarias growing in the shade of the bushes.

A forest of Cephalocereus Hoppenstedtii

A golden Hechtia and some Mammillarias in the scrub

A magnificent branched Myrtillocactus Schenkii near Tehuacan in Mexico

A general view and a cluster of Mammillaria geminispina with a barrel cactus on the hillside at Venados

For our next expedition we travelled for some one hundred miles northward on our way to the Barranca de Venados, to see the home of Cephalocereus senilis (The 'Old Man's Head' cactus). We climbed up the escarpment to find a group of the tall slender Lemaireocereus Dumortieri, as a foreground to a wonderful view over a series of mauvy ravines, not unlike one's first breathtaking view of the Grand Canyon. We drove on a little further towards our ravine, to be shown by my excellent guide (Mr Gold, a prominent American member of the Mexican Cactus Society) some glorious golden Barrel Cacti in a cutting along our road, clinging precariously to the sides of the roadside cliffs. As we photographed him pointing at lovely clusters of deep gold flowers on the top of one of them, he told us that they had not yet been catalogued or named.

Nearby we saw some tiny Dolichothele longimama, growing happily on the ground, before we drove on for our first view of the Cephalocereus senilis. We found them on the steep slopes of the ravine, together with Barrel Cacti (Ferocactus ingens) and white clusters of Mammillaria geminispina, and even a few giant Astrophytum ornatum, quite three feet high. The terrain was stony and very well-drained, and was a pointer to the need to give these plants good drainage at home, to put chippings on top of the pots to avoid collar rot and never to let them get sodden. Some of them were twenty feet high and had glorious white furry heads, and they were certainly very effective, though many were broken and bent from the wind storms which swept the valleys, and some had dirty black 'hair' just as if they had been living in the grime of our big cities. We motored down the slope of the valley below and, in the midst of all these cacti, Mr Gold stopped the car by a small clump of straggly bushes, where to our amazement he said we would find cacti growing as Epiphytes on the trees–and sure enough we have photographs

today of Mammillaria pygaema and Dolichothele longimamma growing in a tiny humid locality on the branches of the trees. It was a surprise to find the Dolichotheles growing in this way, after seeing them thriving as normal cacti on the top of the barranca (ravine).

Another visit to Mexico was one I made with George Lindsay, then head of the Natural History Museum in San Diego, California,–a very knowledgeable man on the plants of Baja California, the peninsula stretching south of San Diego, in the north-west of Mexico. With him we motored through fields of golden Californian poppies, blue lupins, white and yellow daisies and purple verbena to the guest house, with its roof of white shells near El Rosario, some 200 miles from San Diego. After an entertaining communal evening with hunters, travellers and salesmen, we motored for some forty miles over a really rough road, which one could only use as long as one's car ran in the wheel tracks of the local bus. It was an area of barren hillsides with low bushes, parched straggly grass and sandy patches, but to us it was a thrilling place, as on every side there were masses of cactus plants, large and small. The road ran parallel to the sea coast and occasionally we could get a glimpse of the sea when we crossed a hill top or when some of the taller plants were silhouetted against the water of an inlet. There was Agave shawii and Yucca peninsularis, with their tall golden and white flower spikes held high in the air above large fields of the golden Bergerocactus emoryi, in the midst of which we were amazed to see the tiny mauve-pink Rosea minutifolia. We passed a giant Pachycereus Pringlei with clusters of white flowers as we made our way to the land of the Boojum trees (Idria columnaris) which are only to be found in this part of Mexico. Its tall, straight stems are light green in the summer, turning gold as the leaves die off, until in the winter the Boojums are bare and not unlike a silver birch.

Under these rare trees there was the particularly lovely Ferocactus gracilis, with its deep red, curved spines and red-and-white-streaked flowers, whilst on all sides were the tiny grey Mammillaria dioca with its larger white male flowers, looking more effective than the smaller female ones.

On the way home that evening, George Lindsay took us off the road into the sand dunes to search for a tiny Mammillaria which he had seen there several years ago and which was still unnamed. We were lucky as we found it flowering in a mass of small Mesembryanthemum leaves, which for some unaccountable reason were growing in the wild here–far, far away from their native lands of Africa. George Lindsay took home several specimens to send away to botanists to get the plants registered and named. He gave us one which bloomed well later the same year in my collection at Worfield.

Cereus Tetetzo growing in great profusion near Tehuacan in Mexico

**Another fine view of Cephalocereus senilis on
the slopes of the Barranca de Venados in Mexico**

Yucca peninsularis with a tall white flower spike in Baja California

A very old giant Ferocactus ingens on the arid slopes near Tehuacan

A tall Yucca near Techuacan

Cephalocereus senilis in the Barranca de Venados. Note how some are disfigured by the strong winds

An interesting cristate head on a Pachycereus Pringlei

Cephalocereus senilis on the Barranca de Venados

The late Lady Leese with a vast Pachycereus Pringlei

A cluster of Ferocactus on a hillside at Venados

A beautiful group by the roadside of a hitherto unnamed Ferocactus with glorious golden flowers

Mammillaria dioca with its lovely yellow flower with red stripes

My next visit to Mexico was from Tucson, when my kind host Jack Speidon took my wife and me off through Nogales to the attractive fishing and seaside pleasure resort of Guaymas on the Gulf of California. The view at sunrise across the palm trees on the coast over to the islands of the bay has to be seen to be believed. Two charming French people took us out in their boat for a most memorable cruise in the bay, round some of the nearby islands. As we approached one of them, we saw what appeared to be a thick green wood, but as we got closer we saw that these were no trees. They were giant cacti–Pachycereus Pringlei–growing almost down to the water's edge. What an answer this was, once again, to the pundits who tell us that cacti only grow in deserts! The soil on this island was rich and the grass was growing thickly and well, and we soon found other cacti, including Mammillaria dioca, some Ferocactus, Agaves and Chollas, whilst on all sides there were young Pachycereus Pringlei growing on well to replace their elder brethren when their time should come.

We had to drag ouselves away from this island to visit another one, which turned out to be just as interesting but totally different. Here there were more Pachycereus Pringlei, but they were scattered much further apart and were not growing so strongly, and then we noticed that there was no rich soil on this island. The surface was just a tangled mass of rocks, looking as if they had just been dropped out of the sky, and one wondered how any of the plants could find humus on which to survive. Yet in this tumbled mass we found quite big Ferocactus Covillei, surviving all the difficulties. We went on from there for a cruise along the coast. Ahead of us we saw a large, white rock-like island with steep cliffs, just off the coast. Our host told us that it was white with bird-lime from the pelicans which we passed sitting on ledges along the coast. On the sides of this great rock there were tall Pachycereus Pringlei growing tall and strong in the salt spray from the sea.

The yellow Brittle bush with its attractive grey leaves, with an occasional Fouquieria splendens growing like a small bushy tree with its cherry coloured flowers, lined both sides of the road to the frontier at Nogales. We were lucky to see an occasional Paloverde tree in flower with its lovely golden sheen, for when we got further north none of them were in bloom. It was just the same with the Ocotillo and its tall waving wands with the scarlet flowers on their tips. We saw one small clump of these in flower and I stopped to photograph them there, which was lucky, because of the thousands of these plants which we saw as we raced along to Tucson, there were no more in flower.

Two years later I was in Baja California again and accompanied by George Lindsay once more. This time my destination was different: the Bay of Angels on the west coast. It is several hundred

An island off Guaymas with hundreds of Cereus growing right down to sea level

Ocotillo with its fairy-wand-like branches, surmounted by a scarlet flower

Ferocactus Covillei nestling amongst the rocks with its yellow flower on top

Echinocereus Fendleri with its fearsome spines and lovely pink flower

Echinocereus Engelmanii with its deep red flower

Another Echinocereus (called maritimis) with ferocious spines

A lovely golden Echinocereus triglochidiatus with its pink flower

miles from San Diego, so George Lindsay arranged for us to fly down in a chartered light aircraft. It was a very interesting flight, mostly over a barren waterless country, often over scattered trees, with the occasional range of small hills. The Bay of Angels as it appeared on our left was a glorious sight, with the sea a heavenly blue.

We only had to go a short distance from the rest house to realize that we were going to see some most interesting plants. The countryside was dominated by really vast Pachycereus Pringlei. The branching starts three or four feet from the ground. The branches, often thick and long, go almost straight up in the air, and are quite unlike the branches of the Saguaro which assume such fantastic shapes. It is true to say that these two trees are the giants of the Cereus world, just as the Candelabra Euphorbias are in the succulent world of Africa. The tallest Pringlei trees may not be quite as tall as the giant Saguaros, but their trunks seem bigger. They give a terrific impression of size and appear to dwarf an ordinary mortal even more so than the Saguaros. There were, too, a few giant Ferocactus viscicensis, some of them quite six feet tall, slightly leaning as do all the Ferocacti, and with glorious curved red spines. This was also one of the few places where one can find the Elephant tree and the Idria columnaris, known as the Boojum tree. Some of the Idria were quite tall with long elegant narrow stems, covered with spines. The Elephant trees were far more straggly, with branches ranging out in all directions, and with a short, light-coloured trunk. There were, as always in Mexico, some smaller cacti such as Mammillaria dioca and Hutchinsoniana and in one place we saw Lophocereus Schottii sprawling in a tangled mass all over the ground. Occasionally there were Fouquieria peninsularis and the Ocotillo, each with long thin spiny branches with a red flower on the tip, giving an air of grace to their surroundings.

A splendid head of the picturesque Lophocereus Schottii

A lovely red Ferocactus viscisensis almost hidden by the dead wood

The late Lady Leese with a fine red specimen of Ferocactus viscisensis

39

Dudleya Ingens and a Bergerocactus

A magnificent group of Coryphanta erecta with their golden heads

A fine cluster of Mammillaria Sheldonii

A striking branched bush of Myrtillocactus cochal

In their natural habitat

3 South-West Africa

For many years I had been wanting to visit South-West Africa–and it was a very exciting moment when I boarded the aeroplane for Windhoek at Cape Town. Everyone whom we met in South Africa warned me that I was going to the 'White Man's Grave' in South-West, as it would be so hot in January. It certainly was hot sometimes but it was nothing like as stifling and airless as were Kimberley and Pretoria in the heatwave which I encountered later.

Dr Kolle, an enthusiastic succulent collector, took me round and we went first to the Ministry of Agriculture to meet Walter Giess–a great succulent plant expert, and very knowledgeable about their nomenclature. In the open, outside the offices, there was a collection of succulents including a fine Kokobaum tree (Aloe dichotoma) and a beautiful Sycostemma currorii (called Cissus of old) in full flower. Later, at Mr Giess's house, we found a varied and interesting collection of indigenous South African succulents–a great joy to find, as so many people in South Africa in these days have displays in their gardens of American cacti. In point of fact they do extremely well in Africa, but all too seldom do you find gardens of the hardy indigenous succulents for which South Africa is world-famous.

Dr Kolle then took us out to a hillside a short distance from Windhoek. It was a stony outcrop with small thorn bushes. There was a lot of Aloe rubra lutea–four to six feet high, which were coping better than most plants with the lack of rain. There were also many Euphorbia Monteiroi, with its thin green branches, some three feet high with a small red flower on the tips. Then, to our great excitement, we saw Caralluma Niebrownii growing in considerable shade under a thorn bush, with some bush grass protecting it from the sun.

Some twenty miles from Windhoek, towards Kroma reserve, we found an arid countryside: undulating farm land that is not nearly as stony and rocky as it was round Windhoek, with an occasional thorn bush but not trees, and with glorious views over hilly country for miles in every direction.

Dr Kolle at once started to try and find Lithops pseudo-truncatella. Often when we came across them in tiny clumps of at the most four heads, a reddish brown colour, just like the surrounding soil and very low on the ground–one had to brush the dust off them before one could see them properly,

A fine Aloe dichotoma in front of one of the flat-topped hills so typical of South-West Africa

let alone photograph them. He told us that there used to be many more of them, but today they are few and far between, though when you find them there are probably twenty or thirty plants within a few feet of each other. There were a few Aloe hereroensis—greyish in colour and mostly under a foot high—and, to add greatly to our interest, we found a tiny Anacampseros tomentosa hiding under the shade of a thorn bush.

Lithops pseudo-truncatella covered with red dust and almost invisible

Lithops pseudo-truncatella growing very low in the ground near Windhoek

We chartered a light aeroplane, a six-seater American-built Cessna, with a most efficient German pilot who had been in the Luftwaffe during the war. He flew me first to Tsebus to visit the Etosha Pan Game Reserve. The park was not yet officially open, and we stayed in a vast camp in the old German Namutoni Fort. This was famous for a defence by six German soldiers against hordes of Africans. The issue of the fight was touch and go, but at lunch time the Africans broke off the fight to eat, and the German soldiers got on their horses and galloped out of the fort to safety. We then flew on to the attractive seaside resort of Swakopmund, and left next morning in a Land Rover, and right well did we need it. On the tarmac road leading out of the town we soon passed the first tractor to come to South-West Africa, and now a monument to the German colonization. It is a steam affair with a large boiler that looks for all the world like an old muzzle-loading cannon, standing in the place where it finally broke down a few miles from the sea.

Leaving the main road and using the dried-up bed of the Swakop river, we drove to a point where we could work our way up a series of valleys flanked by huge great boulders and rocks, and so into a vast sandy desert. This one great expanse of nothing—just sand, often very soft and sometimes slightly undulating—reminded me of the Qattara depression at El Alamein. Suddenly, the vast desert land flattened out, and we were in the home of the Welwitschias. At first they were black spots in the distance, right up to the horizon. When we came on the first of them, we saw low ugly plants with great sprawling pointed ungainly leaves. Many of them are some three to four foot across and about one foot high in the centre, usually surrounded by dead leaves. Soon we were in the midst of thousands of Welwitschias, alone in a vast sandy waste.

As they were in flower, we could see the male with attractive maroon-coloured flowers, rather as if they were a series of small crosses, and the female with cone-shaped bulbous ones of the same maroon-colour. The bees were busy pollinating them, and in all the débris and rubbish in the midst of the plants there was a kind of red and grey beetle in great profusion.

We motored on to see the giant of the area—an enormous plant some five feet high and much higher than the rest, with a great span of some fifteen to twenty feet across. It is said to be a thousand years old at least, and huge pieces of black driftwood—veritably fossilized—lie in and around the plant. The female plant and the male were a few hundred yards away from each other, whereas in many of the other plants one sees the male and female close together. These plants grow almost nowhere else in the world. It is useless to take a small plant and try to re-root it: it just won't live. You can grow them from seed; they germinate well and you do this on top of a drainpipe, so that the

The male flower of the Welwitschia

The oval female flower of the Welwitschia

The largest Welwitschia, possibly 2000 years old

A fine specimen of Welwitschia

roots can go straight down the pipe as they do in the desert. If you damage any part of the root, the plant will die. The only other place that I know where they are growing successfully in any numbers in cultivation is in the greenhouses of the botanical campus of the University at Stellenbosch in Cape Province. There they were sown many years ago by that great succulent plant botanist, Dr Herre (who drives now at great speed through the university roads with a motor on his chair). The best part of a dozen plants, several feet across, have been taken out of their drainpipes and very carefully re-planted in deep holes in the compost of the greenhouses. Even this has not been too successful.

The next day we flew from Swakopmund in our light aircraft and passed over expanses of sand dunes, landing after three hundred miles at Duwisib, where we spent the night in a castle built by a German at the end of the nineteenth century.

There were no succulents here. It was very dry grassland, in need of rain. Another three hundred miles farther on, at Aus, a small farming town and the rail centre for many miles around, we were met by Mr Erni–a Caracul sheep farmer, who took us out some twenty miles to his farmhouse on a stony outcrop on the hills. Mr Erni is a keen succulent collector–though much of his collection was of American cacti–and he and Mr Giess (who had joined us for this part of our trip) were old friends and were soon well down to it discussing Mr Erni's plants in fluent German. Whilst this was going on, I photographed a fine big Aloe dichotoma next to a Euphorbia dregeana, with its finger-like branches. There was also a large specimen of Euphorbia virosa, which was used by the bushmen to poison their arrows. At last I managed to disengage the two experts and we climbed into a Land Rover to go and have a look at the local succulents growing in the wild. We first saw Lithops kuibisensis with its brown head growing very low in the ground; nearby was Euphorbia lignosa and the squat type Aloe hereroensis. We motored on and then we found the first Saracocaulon I had seen in the wild–Sarcocaulon Patersonii, with its sprawling bonsai-like body. In one small group I photographed this plant with a Euphorbia mauretanica and a Euphorbia–while close by was a Ruschia. We went on a few miles over a rough track through stony hills to find a very dried-up Cotyledon orbiculata, which would have been looked on in shame in any collection at home. We went on a short distance to find Huernia Namaquanum nestling under a small rocky outcrop, and nearby Hereroa Puffkammeriana and the sprawling Pelargonium Xeropayton. We turned for home and lunch and were soon passing Aloe microstigma, reaching our last stop to look for the miniature Titanopsis Lüderitzia–which are literally minute and quite difficult to see.

A fine big bush of Euphorbia Mauretanica, near Rosh Pinah

The tiny Titanopsis Lüderitzia

Euphorbia virosa at Macmillan's Camp on the Orange River

We motored back to the air strip to fly another one hundred and fifty miles down to Rosh Pinah, a new tin mine right out in the blue, about fourteen miles from the Orange River border with South Africa. Everyone had told us that this would be the hottest part of our journey. It was hot by day–but by night it was delightful and one slept with a blanket and wore a warm garment for the first hour or two of the morning.

We stayed in the guest house of the mine with the manager, Jan Botha, a keen succulent collector with a good knowledge of his plants. He was delighted to meet Mr Giess, and the visit turned out to be one of the highlights of my time in South-West. Jan Botha took us out in a Land Rover for a couple of hours before dark. We motored up a track into the hills, a sandy valley with stony and rocky hills on either side. At one point we found the three tall tree like Aloes all in one group–Aloe pillansii, Aloe dichotoma and Aloe ramosissima. I then caught my first sight of a Tricocaulon in the wild. We motored on quickly as the light was starting to fail, to see ahead of us a hillside quite red with the tall maroon red stems of Aloe Pearsonii. The light was getting bad, which was sad as they were in a perfect setting to photograph, next to the same Cotyledon paniculata which you find on the Karoo and near Port Elizabeth. It was a thrilling ending to the day.

We got up in the morning at 5 am for a two-hour outing which became so exciting that we did not get back till 10.30 am. Some twenty miles along the main road, in a heavy morning mist, we turned off and motored three or four miles across country along a boundary fence towards the hills. We stopped after a while to see small clumps, about a foot wide, of Cheiridopsis truncata and another Sarcocaulon, and then we motored up to the foot of the hills. Very soon we were to see the great prize of the day, Aloe erinaceae, which even Mr Giess had never seen before and which was neither named or listed; Jan Botha had discovered it. The individual plant is about a foot high and ten inches across–and they are usually in clumps of up to fifteen plants, in what appears to be a straight line. At this time of year, when there had been no rain, they were a dull green with tinges of mauve and pink.

A real treasury of succulents lay on the hillsides, Kleinia longifolia with its fine long branches, the lovely tree-like Cotyledon dinteri, our old friend Crassula lycopoidioides, and an attractive red Crassula. At the bottom of the hill there was on all sides the bright green Euphorbia mauritanica, and they showed me a Monecama which I had never seen before.

On the way back to the main road we saw the sprawling Pelargonium crithnifolium and Euphorbia namibensis, which grows freely in the Namib desert. We turned back on the main road

The sprawling red leaves of Aloe Pearsonii after a long drought

Jan Botha collecting the rare Aloe erinacea

45

towards Rosh Pinah and then we left the road again to see a magnificent group of tall tree-like Aloe ramosissima, even taller than the one we saw the night before. Near them was Euphorbia gummifera. We returned to camp, very thrilled and much later than we expected, and went straight behind Jan Botha's office to find Sarcostemma siminale and a tall plant of the bulbous Pachypodium namaquense. Outside his office, Jan Botha had collected Othonna opima and Euphorbia hamata, and on the way back to our guest house I photographed Hoodia Bainsei.

A year or so later, again in the summer, I made another visit to South-West Africa. We entered from the south over the Orange River, having left Cape Town in a Cortina and motored up to Springbok, on a hot summer's day. We set out from Springbok at 8.30 am in a Land Rover sent for us by Jan Botha. We drove forty miles along the N11 towards Viooldfrift turning left at Steinkopt along the main road, and another fifty on to Port Nolloth on a graded gravel road, with no villages, just an occasional turning marked off to a farm some miles off the road. There were no cattle or sheep and very little traffic. Nearly all the countryside was sandy desert and we crossed the occasional low range of hills. We saw one Aloe kamisensis and we stopped and photographed one white Namaqualand daisy in flower and a larger edition of the rather sticky Glottiphyllum we had seen near Vredental on our way up. It was fairly hot coming over the desert, and suddenly it turned quite cool and then we saw the sea ahead and over it that same sea mist that we had met at Swakopmund. Port Nolloth had one tiny jetty, but there was a most modern, sophisticated and comfortable hotel.

Next morning we found Jan Botha waiting for breakfast. The mist had prevented him from landing his plane the night before, so he had returned to Rosh Pinah and started again by car at 5 am, to get to us for breakfast—one hundred and twenty miles of dirt roads.

We went a little way back towards Kleinkopt to see Aloe krapoliana, a tiny compact Aloe difficult to find, and later Aloe arenicola spreading all over the place, not unlike Aloe Pearsonii. We then started off towards Rosh Pinah, some one hundred and thirty miles of gravel road. After a few miles we saw Aloe framesii, sprawling again like Aloe Pearsonii. Each of these last three Aloes appeared just in one small area in small numbers.

We next turned down to the sea, to find an eerie beach of rocks and floating sea-weed. Inland we found some attractive brown and green lichen, and where there was some water, some Mesembryanthemums in flower. We passed two outposts of the diamond industry, all out of bounds and obviously guarded, and we saw some interesting tree-like Pelargoniums. We travelled over sandy desert to reach the Orange River, where it was several hundred yards across, with plenty of water

coming down. No effort was being made to exploit the water, and one thought of the wonders of what is being done with the Jordan water in Israel.

We continued across this desert and we found a small kopje with Euphorbia namibensis some small Tricocaulon, Conyphytums and Anacampseros, a fine variety. We moved on to Cornells Kop, where they had told us to see some forty Aloe pillansii, some up to forty feet high, a really lovely sight. A little later there were large clumps of Aloe ramosissima, as usual a bushy-type tree growing low and circular.

I saw quite a lot of the Richtersveld, a big area mentioned in several books as the home of many succulents. In the north, the border follows the Orange River from Sendlingsdrift to Vioolsdrift, and then runs south to Steinkopt and west to Port Nolloth. We were now to have an exciting glimpse of a tract of country which I doubt if any other English people have visited. We went along a track constructed a few years ago by a South African called Macmillan, who was making a scientific survey. He took some two years over it, with four-wheel-drive vehicles and a few boys. We went out of Rosh Pinah about 7.30 am, very sensibly taking two Land Rovers in case of trouble. We motored out in an easterly direction across the plain for some ten miles seeing the occasional isolated Aloe dichotoma, and suddenly we were confronted by a perpendicular track, which had none of the sweeping curves of the modern hill climb, but went quite straight up. It was just broad enough for the Land Rovers, and up we went, the second one waiting till we got up. They both came up magnificently and at the top I photographed some bright red Aloe garipensis, as before in a locality with just a few plants. They were nice-sized single heads growing low on the ground. Nearby were some attractive little bonsai-looking small beech-type trees. We went on over wild, hilly country, never seeing a soul, not even a donkey, but we were lucky enough to see two gemsbok, two springbok and four klipspringers leaping from rock to rock up what looked like sheer precipices. All along the route were Euphorbias of the mauretanica type and small Senechios, Kalanchoes and Crassulas. We then passed groups of large, spreading light-green Euphorbia avasmontana. They had long branches up to six feet in height, fanning out and remaining quite upright—usually a dozen or so plants together, at frequent intervals along our route.

There was the occasional tall Aloe pillansii and Aloe dichotoma and a mass of lovely low umbrella-type Aloe ramoisissima, all in very good condition. We went along river beds, and at this part of our journey made only some eight miles in the hour. The drivers had to be very careful not to knock the bottom of the car on one of the rocks in the road way. We saw a few Hoodia Bainsei, looking rather straggly and up to eighteen inches high. There were

Aloe Pearsonii showing through a parched thicket

The top of a sheer direct climb up the mountain side en route for the Orange River

Aloe ramosissima, with its low curved branches, near Rosh Pinah

Aloe Pearsonii, with its leaves reddened by the drought, at sunset

Euphorbia avasmontana in the river bed, on the way to Macmillan's Camp

A lovely branched Euphorbia with red seed pods

Pachypodium Namaquensis. It is unusual to find one of them branched

Frances Denby examining the head of a Pachypodium Namaquensis

A typical shaped clump of Aloe erinacea, in a straight row

The sprawling Aloe Pearsonii at sunset

Hoodia Gibbosa in full flower

Ceraria-type plants and black-looking Pelargoniums and suddenly we came on the 'Half Men', Pachypodium namaquensis. It was a great thrill to see them up high on a cliff side, some like sentinels on the top—up to ten feet in height and, luckily, one or two lovely ones lower down, where I could photograph them. All bending slightly to the north, with their green tip on top, as usual broader at the bottom, narrowing to the point, with brown bodies full of thorns.

We looked back from a little hill top, and saw the blue Land Rover in obvious trouble. We went back. The fan had slipped and made a hole in the radiator, and was running the water out. There was nothing we could do, so we put everyone, with all our lunch, into *our* Land Rover and on we went. Anyhow we were almost at the Orange River, and we halted by Macmillan's camp, to see Euphorbia virosa, about a dozen big plants, also branching from the ground in tall darker green branches, and more crinkled than the Euphorbia avasmontana. We were careful not to touch them, as they were used in the old days by the locals to make the poison for their poisoned arrows. Near Macmillan's camp we found the skin covering of a golf ball with a succulent growing out of it! As we looked at all this, we felt that Macmillan deserved the honours award he was subsequently given at Cape Town University.

We motored on a mile or two over sandy flats to a lovely spot with shady trees on the banks of the Orange River, which was a full hundred yards wide and obviously deep in the middle.

There was quite a dust storm which blew over everything. After a barbecue lunch, we started back to the blue Land Rover. Over this country it was a terrific strain for our one to tow the other vehicle, which to make matters worse had a flat tyre. Soon ours began to heat up and Jan Botha decided to leave the blue one behind and send out a team to deal with it later. So we all piled in to our Land Rover again, and we got to the top of the hill and looked down into the plain. We dug up the stunted 'bonsai' trees, and then went down the hill in first gear with the engine ticking over. It was a tough descent, and the plain below in the soft, failing light looked to us just like the Promised Land.

Photographs of some fifty plants which are recommended as suitable for anyone starting a general collection follow on pages 50-83. Each specimen is described, with useful comments for the novice grower. Further advice on making collections of various kinds will be found on pages 120-140.

The chapter **In their natural habitat** continues on page 84

Selected plants for a collection

Agave Americana variegata

Agaves are natives of the New World, from the southern states of the USA to Mexico, Central America and the Caribbean. There are over 300 species. They were imported in ballast into the Mediterranean area, where they are so numerous that they are considered as indigenous. Sometimes known as the Century Plant, they only flower after some seven years, with a fine golden head on a twenty-foot stem. They then die, but leave behind plenty of offsets to perpetuate the species. In a really large collection they can grow to a large and most impressive size. In smaller collections, the young plants are most useful. Agave Americana variegata is particularly effective with yellow and green-striped leaves, which are used for sisal and, in Mexico, for preparing the drinks of pulque and tequila.

Right: Aporocactus flagelliformis see page 52
Below: Cereus Peruvianus see page 53

Aloe

Nearly 300 species of Aloe come from Africa and Arabia. Some grow to heights of over ten feet, particularly Aloe Bainsei, which at Port Elizabeth in South Africa is a good fifty feet high. At the other end of the scale, there are the miniature ones, particularly attractive when they are in flower. Aloe aristata is one of these. One of the best known for a collection is Aloe variegata, known as the Partridge Breasted Aloe. A full-grown plant may be one foot tall. The leaves are dark green, irregularly banded with whitish markings. The edges of the leaves are hard and have teeth. The plant bears reddish flowers on a comparatively short flower spike. Propagation of Aloe variegata is slow from offshoots, but seeds germinate quite well. Some Aloes, such as Aloe vera, have been used for medicinal purposes. The larger Aloes bear tall and elegant gold and red flower spikes.

Aporocactus flagelliformis

This native of Mexico (where it hangs down from rocks and trees) has pendant clusters of very attractive crimson flowers, which are open for several days. It can also be effective if grafted on a stock of Selenicereus or Harrisii.

Astrophytum

The Star Cactus, also often known as the Bishop's Cap, because of its five, acute, spineless ribs. It originated in Mexico. Astrophytum are in most cases dotted with scales that are really minute hairs, whitish grey in colour, making the plant look like a stone. The flowers are yellow, sometimes with a crimson patch at the base. They are borne singly and are quite large for the size of the plant. Flowers continue to come into bloom for some time in succession. They seldom produce offsets, but propagate easily from seeds. Do not plant them too deeply, as rot may set in.

Cephalocereus senilis

There are at least seventy species, mostly from Mexico and South America. They often grow to be large plants, with rather dull, small flowers. Their attraction lies in the long wool and hair growing from the areole and often the top of the flowering stem. This extra mass of hair is known as a cephalium and is one of the genus's distinguishing features.

The best known is Cephalocereus senilis, which comes from the Barranca de Venados which can be visited in a day from Mexico City. It is known as the Old Man Cactus. It is a slow-growing plant with long white hairs. Often it is unbranched and some twenty feet high. Sometimes it has several branches. Their home is on a well-drained slope, and the mature plants stand up snow-white against the bluc sky, but some of the older ones are quite black and multi-headed as the result of the damage done by the winds that sweep the slopes. The red and white flowers appear during the night, but I have not yet seen one flower in England. They propagate easily from seed. They need good drainage and it is best to put chippings on top of the compost to stop collar rot.

Cereus

Over 20 species. Comes mostly from South America, and is named after the Latin word for a torch. They are tall and columnar and usually have no hairs. They do not flower till they are several feet high. They have large flowers, often white and scented, sometimes pink resembling water lilies. They open during the night and if the weather is hot they start to die off before midday. Cereus Peruvianus is a strong-growing hardy plant, which is easy to propagate either from cuttings or from seed. As a background plant, it gives height to a display or to a bowl garden.

Cereus Peruvianus monstrosus

From South America. Grows up to 30 feet in height, with bluish stems up to eight inches thick. It is a cristate (or crested) plant, and the branches are also crested. Cuttings usually perpetuate the cristate form, and seeds sometimes do so. It is known as the Rock Cactus, as there are small oval projections on the stem which make it resemble a bluish rock face. It has a large trumpet-shaped flower – very lovely in its colouring, brownish-green on the outside of the outer petals, reddish at the tips and white on the inside, with white inner petals. Cereus Jamacaru also has a cristate form.

Conophytum see page 56

Cotyledon orbiculata see page 57

Crassula lycopodioides variegata see page 57

Chamaecereus silvestrii

From western Argentina. It is a miniature cactus and is the only species of the Chamæcereus. It is a small, sprawling, prostrate plant, often grown in a shallow pan, over which it can crawl about at will.

The flowers are scarlet, about two inches long and very decorative. During the growing season it likes a lot of sunshine and plenty of water. Easy to grow from cuttings.

Cleistocactus Straussii

Cleistocactus Straussii

Known as the Silver Torch, because it is completely covered with slender glassy-white spines. The areoles are filled with tufts of white wool, with thin, white bristles. They originated in Bolivia, where they grow to some four feet, and do not branch unless they are damaged. They have disappointing flowers when they are two to three feet high: a small red tube with violet petals along the stem of the plant. They grow easily from seeds; offshoots develop at the base. The plant is a very decorative addition to any collection and they do very well in miniature gardens.

Conophytum

There are 250 species from South-West Africa and South Africa. They are known as the Cone Plants. They are one of the smallest Mesembryanthemums and are very attractive, with their small juicy bodies through which brilliantly coloured flowers emerge in autumn. After the rains, they are an attractive bluey-green colour, and in times of drought, when they are exposed to the full sun, the plants turn a deep russet crimson. They grow on ground level and also in crevices on the rocks and on cliff faces.

They flower at a different time from Lithops: from August to October, sending a long thin flower stem through the slit at the top. The flowers may be yellow, pink or violet. New plant bodies form each year inside the old ones, which slowly shrivel and die. Give them a little water in March when the new body is being formed. They store this water for the next dry period. From May until they show some life in July or August, give them no water. They grow well from seed or from divisions.

Cotyledon orbiculata

Cotyledons are mostly succulent shrubs or semi-shrubs from South-West Africa and South Africa, which are usually easy to grow. During droughts in their native haunts they become black and look as if they must die, yet when the rains come they come to life again and flower in a seemingly miraculous way. Cotyledon orbiculata comes from Cape Province. It is a strong-growing grey plant. Its silvery-white leaves have a lovely sheen and red edges. Its bell-shaped, golden-yellow flowers hang from a long stalk. Cotyledon undulata, a very lovely small plant, also comes from Cape Province in South Africa. The leaves have a silvery-white bloom with a glorious sheen. The leaves are oval with a wavy edge. Its graceful bell-shaped flowers are yellowish red. It is difficult to grow, as it is

prone to rot off. It likes some shade in summer, but full light in winter, and a moderate amount of water all the year. It is a most decorative and highly prized addition to any collection.

Crassula lycopodioides variegata

Another very useful plant for small arrangements and bowl gardens. It resembles a small tree with tiny, closely-perched ivy-green leaves along the whole length of the stem and branch. It is easily grown and propagates well from cuttings. The silver-grey variety, Crassula lycopodioides variegata, is particularly attractive.

Crassula falcata is another attractive species with a lovely red flower. Crassula Schmidtii is also a useful small plant which flowers easily in the late autumn, and so is very useful for bowl gardens. There are also many miniature Crassulas, which would make a good collection on their own.

Crassula portulacea

The Crassulas mostly come from Africa and there are over 200 species. Crassula portulace originated in Cape Province. When fully grown, they are fine big bushes up to six feet in height, flowering with a little, rather insignificant pink flower. The smaller plants are easy to keep under control and make excellent backgrounds for all sizes and sorts of collections and displays. It is easy to take the cuttings, which root easily. These are tough plants that stand up to hard conditions.

Echeveria derenosa *var.* **Worfield Wonder**
see page 60

Echeveria derenosa
var. Worfield Wonder

There are over 500 species of Echeveria, originally from Central and North America. They are very beautiful succulents, many of which can safely be used for bedding out. Echeveria derenosa (Worfield Wonder) is a lovely hybrid of my own growing, which has been given the Award of Merit of the Royal Horticultural Society. Its short, blue-green leaves have a waxy surface which always keeps clean and shining. It has bell-shaped red and yellow flowers carried on a short compact flower spike which never gets straggly. It blooms in March and April and so is an excellent pot plant, but it flowers too early for bedding. It produces many offsets, which root easily.

Echeveria gibbiflora metallica is a useful tall plant in much demand for flower arrangement. It has a beautiful pink-and-bronze-coloured leaf.

Echinocactus Grusonii

A most impressive Barrel Cactus from Mexico. It is circular and usually grown as a solitary ball. It also grows in magnificent clusters, particularly if any part of the plant is damaged. It has the most fearsome golden spines and is rather unkindly known as Mother-in-Law's Chair. One hundred-year-old single plants are a wonderful sight.
It bears rather insignificant yellow flowers on the top, but needs plenty of hot sun to make it bloom. It is a valuable addition to any collection and is particularly useful in the golden section of large arrangements.

Echeveria setosa

A very beautiful plant. It has large, single rosettes with narrow, rounded, dark-green leaves covered with fine white bristles. It is a good spring and summer plant for bedding and as a pot plant. Its flowers are reddish yellow in early spring. Echeveria pulvinata, especially the variety Ruby, is another attractive plant, the colouring of which varies from silver to a vivid green tipped with bright red in the winter.

Echinopsis

Originated in South America, and is often known as the Easter Lily cactus. Round or elongated, rather similar in appearance to Lobivias, but often bigger. The flowers are long or trumpet-shaped on long tubes, hairy, scaly and scented in some species. The flowers last only a few days but are very decorative. Most species are pink, but some are white or yellow. They have many offsets, which propagate easily. More resistant to cold than most cacti, they can often be grown in cold greenhouses.

Top: Echeveria setosa see page 60   **Bottom: Echinocactus Grusonii** see page 60

Euphorbia obesa

An interesting Euphorbia of a totally different shape. It is small and round, and sometimes rather taller than it is broad. It is very similar to Euphorbia valida or Euphorbia meloformis, but it is otherwise quite unlike any other Euphorbia. Apart from ribs and grooves, it is quite smooth, with none of the thorns on most other Euphorbias. It came originally from one farm near Port Elizabeth in South Africa. It has insignificant green flowers. It propagates from seed and it is wise to put muslin over the plant when the seed is ripening, as it may be ejected some distance.

Euphorbia splendens

There are over 350 species of almost every conceivable size and shape. Most of them originated in Africa. Many of them have an insignificant yellow flower. Euphorbia splendens, however, has an attractive scarlet flower. It is a native of Madagascar and cannot stand up to even the slightest frost. It is an attractive, slow-growing shrub, known as the Christ's Thorn or the Crown of Thorns. The flowers mostly appear in the spring, but they can also appear throughout the year. The leaves may fall off, but this need not cause alarm. It likes plenty of water.

Euphorbia Tananarive

A very attractive yellow variety from Madagascar, which will not stand up to frost. It usually flowers in the spring and many last for a considerable time. There is also an attractive branched variety called Euphorbia candelabra, which is very useful as a background in arrangements.

If you are working with Euphorbias, be careful not to let the white milky liquid from a damaged stem get into your eyes or mouth.

Fenestraria

Known as the Babies' Toes, and comes from South-West Africa. It is a stemless succulent, with translucent tops or 'windows'. The plant buries itself underground with only the windows showing, through which the sunlight penetrates so that the plant can carry out the normal food-making processes in its leaves, even though they are buried. The flowers have short stalks, with slender petals—yellow on Fenestraria aurantiaca and white on Fenestraria rhopalophylla. They need a lot of light or they may damp off; water sparingly, but frequently.

Epiphyllum

There are now over 3000 named hybrids in cultivation. The original 16 species of Epiphyllum originated in the warm, humid, tropical jungles of Central and South America. They bore white flowers, intensely fragrant, which appeared during the night and drew the insects to them for pollination. They have been hybridized so that now they bear flowers of every conceivable hue. They are a lovely plant to possess when they flower in the spring, though for the rest of the year the long, notched and toothed stems are dull and uninteresting.

Espostoa lanata

Originated in Peru. They are a columnar plant with rounded ribs, white hair and wool and a pseudocephalium at the top of the flowering stems, from which emerge the small, funnel-shaped flowers. The hairs are fine and silky and cover the entire body. Espostoa lanata is a particularly beautiful species with its shining white, matted, silk-like hairs entirely covering the body. It needs the same treatment as Cephalocereus senilis, as it is liable to get collar rot. It is a great asset in a white group in a large arrangement. The small plants are also attractive.

Faucaria

Known as the Tiger's Jaw. Originated in the Karoo in South Africa. Along the top edges of the tough boat-shaped leaves there is a row of teeth that curves back and ends in a fine point. This gives the plant the look of a fierce animal's jaw. Before Christmas, there is a large, brilliant yellow flower. It grows very easily from seed and is a useful plant in collections and bowl gardens.

Kalanchoë tomentosa

There are at least 200 species of Kalanchoë, coming from Africa, India and the Far East. They are from damper climates than most succulents and like more water in the summer. They make good plants and have attractive flowers. Kalanchoë tomentosa–known as the Panda plant–is a most beautiful type. It has greenish-white, felted leaves of a silvery sheen and has brown markings on the edges. There are also some large plants such as Kalanchoë behairensis, which I have seen in Kenya six feet high in large bushes of lovely velvety leaves, grey outside and brownish-gold inside.

Gymnocalycium group

There are some 50 species from South America. They are known as the Chin Cactus as they have a distinctive chin beneath the areoles. They are small plants, circular and grooved and with ribs. They flower very well, with pinkish white flowers on top which seem rather large for the size of the plant. They are very strong and like a well-drained compost; not too much water in the winter but plenty in the summer, when the flowers are produced.

Gymnocalycium pungens

Hamatocactus setispinus

From Texas and Mexico. A useful plant for any collection. There are only three species. It is a small, round plant, easy to cultivate and free-flowering, rather later in the summer than most flowering cacti. Hamatocactus setispinus has attractive yellow flowers, funnel-shaped and on short stems. There are notches on the ribs and whitish spines. They do well in bowl gardens. See colour picture on page 70.

Harrisii

Comes from South America. They are tall, thin plants that sprawl. They start by being erect but as they lengthen they become prostrate and produce slender branches, which have spines. They flower at night with scented flowers up to eight inches long. The flowers are followed by red rounded fruit with spiney surfaces. Harrisii bonplandii is another useful plant and is often used as a stock on which to graft Zygocactus.

Above and top right: Harrisii

Kleinia tomentosa

There are 44 species of Kleinias, which originated in Africa, the Canary Islands and India. Kleinia tomentosa is most attractive, growing as an upright shrub about one foot high, with branches that start upright and may go prostrate as the plant ages. It is covered with a beautiful silvery-white felt, with minute silky hairs. It needs careful growing and dislikes excessive watering. It does not often flower and is a 'collector's plant' because of the beauty of its leaves. Avoid spilling water on the leaves and branches, as they are easily marked.

Opposite, bottom left: Hamatocactus setispinus scc pagc 69
Opposite, bottom right: Lobivia see page 72
Below: Mammillaria Zeilmanniana see page 73

Notocactus concinnus

There are twenty-five species of Notocactus from
South America. They are easy to grow and are one
of the most satisfactory additions to a collection.
They are mostly smallish, round and flat-topped
and the red and yellow flowers come from the top
and are large for the size of the plant. Once
started, they flower freely each year. Notocactus
concinnus, Notocactus Ottonis and Notocactus
mammulosus are all very similar and flower well.

Opuntia microdasys albispina

There are three types of these attractive plants. The ordinary yellow one, the white one known as Opuntia microdasys albispina and the red one known as Opuntia microdasys rufida. They are more tender than most Opuntias, and get spotted if they are exposed to cold or to strong winds. They are covered with tiny glochids, which the novice often does not notice, and which can prove very irritating and even unpleasant. They are a valuable asset to any collection. They are usually unsuitable in miniature gardens, where they are inclined to get too much water and so rot off.

Notocactus group

A group of Notocactus in flower is a valuable addition to any collection. Another member of this family is Notocactus Leminghausii, which is usually a larger plant, and is a beautiful golden cactus from Brazil. It is rather a slow grower and may reach three feet high. It is a particularly useful plant in a golden group with Echinocereus Grusonii. It usually does not flower till it is nine to ten inches high. Then the flowers are borne on the top and may be two inches wide, a gloriously golden group effect.

Notocactus scopa

It has very pretty, soft, white, fir-like spines, sometimes with red centrals. It needs care when it is young, as it may damp off. It flowers freely with a yellow flower. Another rather similar plant is Notocactus Haselbergii, a very lovely plant which may take several years to start flowering, but once started has beautiful orange-scarlet flowers which last six weeks.

Opuntia - Prickly Pear

Commonly known as the Prickly Pear, it originated in North and South America. Many Opuntias eventually grow too large for the ordinary collector – but at any time pads can be cut off and rooted quite easily to form new, small plants. You find them all over the world and in many countries they are now treated as indigenous, though they almost certainly came over from America in the sixteenth century. They are very easy to grow and form excellent background plants in arrangements of any size. They will flower if they have plenty of sun, usually yellow, sometimes red.

Oreocereus trollii

From Peru and Bolivia. It has dense cream or grey
wool, which entirely covers the stem and from
which white spines emerge. It is known as the Old
Man of the Andes. Oreocereus celsianus is a
beautiful cactus which in its native habitat may
reach three feet high. They often form clumps, as
the stems branch low down. It is difficult to see the
shape of the ribbed stem, as it is so thickly clothed
with silky white hairs, which nearly hide the long,
yellowish spines. It needs careful watering and
will not stand damp or drips. Both species bear
brownish-red flowers with long tubes.

Parodia

From South America and Mexico. Twenty-eight
species. A small, round, elongated plant with
strong, well-defined ribs, varying a lot in
appearance with white, yellow or brown spines.
They propagate easily from seeds. They are free-
flowering, mostly with red or yellow flowers—
borne near the top of the plant. Parodia aureispina,
Parodia chrysacanthion, Parodia Maasii and
Parodia nivosa, are all good flowerers.

Pleiospilos

Known as the Granite plants. They originated in Cape Province in South Africa. There are several species, of which Bolusii is the best known, with broad, half-round leaves with wrinkled ends. The colour is brownish-green, spotted with dark green. The flowers are yellow in twos or threes. They are larger than most of the stone plants. They are easy to grow, but they do not like too much water in winter and early spring. If they are grown hard in full sun, they will develop their true shapes, but if they have too much water they may develop out of shape.

Left: Selenicereus see page 81
Above: Zygocactus truncatus see page 83

Rebutia Marsoneri

A very effective plant with strong, yellow flowers. In a group, it makes an excellent foil to the red varieties. Rebutia Kesselringiana is another useful plant, with pale yellow flowers. Like the red varieties, they flower at the bottom of the stem, and are worthy of a place in any collection. Rebutia violaciflora is another lovely variety with violet flowers. Rebutias do very well in bowl gardens.

Right: Rebutia Kesselringiana

Rebutia miniscula

A small, roundish plant from South America. It often flowers when quite young and small. Rebutias are very free-flowering, with flowers appearing in great profusion from the base of the stem. They last for several days, closing up at night and opening in the morning. They stand up to full sunshine, but the flowers will last longer if partially shaded. They need plenty of water. Rebutia senilis is also a free-flowering plant with red flowers.

Schlumbergera

Known as the Easter or China cactus. Lovely, wide flowers, with many pendant curved scarlet petals, bloom in the spring. In its native Brazilian jungles, it appears like other Epiphytes in the tops of the trees where the air is moist and the humus in the crotches is lime-free. In cultivation, give them plenty of humus and no lime. They like plenty of water during their growing and flowering periods. They need at all times a warm, moist atmosphere with good drainage. The plants look well when grafted on some stock like Selenicereus Macdonaldii, which does not go dormant when the Schlumbergera is flowering.

Selenicereus

Known as the Moon cactus, it originated in Texas, Mexico and South America. There are twenty-five species, of which the best known is Selenicereus grandiflorus, called the Queen of the Night. They are night-flowering and have the most lovely, big, scented flowers. The flowers are white with variously-coloured backs. The rather slender ribbed stems branch very freely and growth is remarkably quick on established specimens. They can be trailed effectively up the uprights in the greenhouse and then they can be trained overhead along wires. They can also be grown in big pots if they are carefully bent round canes fixed in the pots.

Stapelia

Known as the Starfish flower, it originated in
Central and Southern Africa. There are over a
hundred species and many varieties. They are
strange fleshy plants of reddish-brown or green
colouring. The flowers are spectacular, with five
petals, exotic in their colouring. They look like
wrinkled printed fabric with intricate patterns in
purple browns, velvety blacks and clear yellows,
sometimes fringed with silky hairs.

Stapelia variegata has beautiful flowers but it
does give off a horrid smell, which attracts the
flies. Hopeful of finding carrion, they come and
pollinate the flowers.

Titanopsis

Originated in South Africa. There are seven
species. They are quaint little stemless succulents,
growing in clumps. The russet-grey leaves are
studded with raised dots, some pale grey and some
reddish. They look like small pieces of Tufa rock.
The flowers are bright yellow and orange. They do
not like too much water, but as much sun as
possible.

Trichocereus

A particularly attractive plant with yellow to
brown spines on light green stems. Originated in
South America. They are tall, columnar, branching
plants, some with very long spines with very large,
white flowers, which usually open at night with a
very sweet scent. They are funnel-shaped and
appear near the top of the plant. They usually fade
before noon. I have seen them used for fences in
Mexico, where they are particularly lovely when
the flowers are out. They are useful as a grafting
stock.

Zygocactus truncatus

Originated in the Organ Mountains and other ranges near Rio de Janeiro in Brazil. It is known as the Crab or Christmas cactus and is thought to have been in cultivation since 1918. It has small, many-jointed flat stems and teeth at the joints. These plants make excellent hanging subjects and, when grafted on some stem such as Selenicereus, they form attractive and graceful umbrella-shaped specimens. They have long, carmine flowers, somewhat like those of a Fuchsia. They like a little shade in the summer and only a little water. They need plenty of water when the buds begin to form. They flower before and after Christmas. When looking after Zygocactus, it is important to remember that they originally came from the forests, where they lived high up in the jungle trees, in extremely humid conditions but with excellent drainage.

Zygocactus Rudolph Zenneck

A most useful and effective plant with lovely fat crimson flowers. It was originally hybridized in Germany—probably by Johannes Nicolai in Dresden. During World War I he lost many of his plants, but we probably still have a few of his hybrids which were reproduced after the war, this time at the Beahm Gardens in California. One of the strongest of these hybrids is Zygocactus Königerwcihnachtsfreude, which blooms profusely with pointed orange flowers. There is also Zygocactus delicatus which has a narrow white flower tinged with pink. These all flower in November and December.

In their natural habitat

4 South Africa in summer

To see how plants survive in the scorching sun and a complete drought, and photograph them in these conditions, I was told one had to go to South Africa in the summer, but people told me I must be mad to go there at that time of year, and I even began to doubt the wisdom of making such a trip myself, but in the end it was a great success. The temperatures were high, and riding up river beds in a Land-Rover can be pretty tough, but my friends and I survived and enjoyed it, and we were rewarded with a most interesting experience.

After two days of every kind of emotion at the Newlands Test Match between Australia and South Africa, we set forth in a Cortina to do the 400 miles to Springbok, equipped for the worst: a water bag outside our radiator, an ice bag for our food and drink, enough drink for an army corps and every kind of foodstuff and fruit, to say nothing of two Thermoses with iced water. Except for a 20-mile stretch some ten miles short of Springbok,

where they are making a new road over the hills, there is an excellent tarmac road. At Clanwilliam we went out to Park Huis up the mountainside road to try, with no success, to find a miniature Aloe, but we did see some interesting Euphorbias, growing with small branched arms in clumps at ground level, and also some remarkable rock effects – huge round boulders which were to dominate the scene for the next hundred miles. It had been a really hot day, and we were beginning to wonder if we would be able to take it, but we were reassured when the locals said it was the hottest day they remembered, and they certainly were showing it just as much as we were.

Towards Vredendal, we saw quite a lot of succulents, mostly in very parched farmland, and occasional scrub and Namaqualand daisies – all black and utterly dry. There were some Cotyledons and Kalanchoës looking very dry, but in flower and some small Crassulas by the roadside.

The land of the 'Half-men Cacti' near Springbok

We had an interesting hour or so, and then the motor started to miss. It was Sunday and everywhere was deserted except for little black children going to Church, very well dressed and in hats. We had passed Vredendal and were at a little cross-road by a small group of houses at Koependaan, but luck was with us. We knocked up the garage owner of an unpromising-looking place. He was quite charming and though he had no previous experience with Cortinas, he found out, after about two hours, that the choke was jamming on the carburettor and eventually got it right. On a very long thirty miles on dirt road we saw just one interesting thing: a collection on both sides of the road of Aloe Pearsonii in flower with a red spine. The plants were a maroon red and bent in all directions like those I had seen at Rosh Pinah in South-West Africa. We stopped at Bitterfontein, lunching in the shade under some roofing at the railway station, where there was a nice bed of succulents, and drove on, crossing the Oliphant River, with some water in it. Along the twenty-mile stretch, where they are turning the final stages into tarmac, we struck some fine red Aloes and a few Carpobrotus at the side of the road. There was a big clump of Aloes, and as we crossed the hills quite a lot of the tree Aloe dichotoma. We then got on to more tarmac, to see a few Aloe melanocantha a mile or so short of Springbok.

The tall, tree-like Aloe dichotoma in an utterly parched desert land

Sprawling clumps of Euphorbias at Clanwilliam

A fine Aloe dichotoma standing like a sentinel amidst the rocks

The next morning, Mr Dumoulay, a Belgian and curator of the nature conservation reserve picked us up in a Land-Rover and took us straight into the reserve a few miles out of Springbok. It is large, with some 30,000 acres of mountains and hillsides made up of vast boulders, some cracked – they seemed to have fallen out of the skies. Many of them were perched perilously one on top of the other. They are all rounded and you feel that at some time they must have been under the sea. We saw a lot of the tree-like Aloe dichotoma, which is most effective standing up against the sky on one of these features. We saw some giant Cotyledons, the biggest I had ever seen, and took the seed of a tiny Cheiridopsis. Otherwise there was not much in the reserve, which was utterly parched and dry after practically no rains for two years. The smaller plants had sunk under the ground in self-protection. The Nature Conservation Establishment, set up in recent years, is very orderly, with a black staff of some thirty. Near the Dumoulays' house there was a long, slatted house with all kind of succulents, including an excellent collection of local Stapelias, and a lot of seedlings which had germinated well. It was most efficient, with a mist spray and plenty of water. Outside, there was a mixed bed of large succulents, with interesting tall local Aloes.

In the late afternoon we motored past two of the vast copper mines which are rising up all round here. At first we went through the usual rocky round boulder area, as we did in the morning, and then we entered a vast area of very stony mountains, with desert sandy wastes below. Everywhere amongst the stones and boulders were scorched, Namaqualand daisies, some dead, and occasionally one saw lovely red and green thin-stemmed Euphorbias – looking fresh in contrast to the black-burnt Cotyledons and Kalanchoës. We wondered how they could ever come to life again.

We found some large clumps of Cheiridopsis looking incredibly blue-green and alive, considering the drumming of drought they had been through. We passed an occasional native hut, often of corrugated iron, until we found a kind of nomad tribe living in fascinating round huts, all made of sacking. They were miles from nowhere and had to walk thirty-five miles to Springbok to buy anything. They looked very happy and cheerful, and lived in the midst of this awful drought on the few sheep and goats they owned. A local girl was ill, and so we took her into Springbok, in the back of the Land-Rover with two black workers from the Nature Conservation Establishment and two vast Aloes they had collected. One of these was Aloe khamisensis, a tall red Aloe standing some eight feet high, which grows in small groups of just a dozen or so plants in one area on a little kopje, where they look lovely up against the sky.

A tall Aloe khamisensis against the bright blue sky

The Curator of the Nature Reserve with a fine Aloe khamisensis

A fine tall Aloe khamisensis looking very parched after the drought

Parched specimens of Aloe khamisensis which have flowered despite the drought

To find Aloe glauca, a small grey-green Aloe growing on top of a hillside, we motored down the opposite slope of the valley, and then for several miles along a very rocky river bed, and up a mountainside strewn everywhere with rocks. It was a great feat by the Land-Rover—and eventually we saw Aloe glauca—again only some thirty or so plants, mixed up with a few Cotyledons and, what was rather fun, two clumps of Stapelia hottentorium. On the top of this mountain, to my complete surprise, we came on an excellent dirt track road, and did the twenty-five miles back to Springbok.

The next morning we visited a garden in the town belonging to Mr Van Heerden, aged seventy-six and a 'retired school master'. He had a really magnificent collection of plants from South-West Africa and from Namaqualand, with a few from Kenya and other parts of Africa. He has only bought one plant in all his years of collecting. He must have had several thousand plants, all looking very well, and despite the shortage here he has plenty of water. His range of Aloes is immense, including lovely great dichotoma and ramosissima. His Lithops look very good—much bigger than usual, but they do not look blown up. The best of it all is that, for once, his is not a collection of plants in rows of pots, but is all arranged as a most attractive garden in beds, with nothing but succulents, except for some twenty cacti, against the background of Bougainvillia on his white house.

Next morning we started off once more in the Land-Rover with Mr Dumoulay and two African boys, armed with sacking and every imaginable tool for taking plants. We went some forty miles on the tarmac road to Steinkopt and then out along the road towards Port Nolloth, to a gateway into a vast African reserve. We saw practically no cultivation, partly because of the drought, but the reserve seems very sparsely populated and the natives just run goats and a few sheep. We started off over easy sandy tracks and we began at once to see a mass of most interesting plants. We had seen little up to now on the way out from Springbok, except for one glorious collection of fifty or more Aloe dichotoma, on a hillside quite close to the road, but now we were right in the middle of it. Everywhere were Namaqualand daisies and often Cotyledons—mostly living and just waiting to burst into flower and greenery if only the rain would come.

Soon we came across lovely green plants of Cheiridopsis, often in great clumps through which you could hardly walk without treading on one of them. It was interesting to observe them like this and understand why they should look so well and blue-green when everything else was parched and black. Amongst them was an occasional Stapelia hottentotorium, black and dry in that open sunlight which day after day becomes inexorable to humans, animals and plants alike. Even to us, it began to

seem as if the summer had no end, but then we reminded ourselves that by contrast at home in England we seldom have two days running on which we can look out at breakfast and be quite certain that it would not cloud over or rain that day.

We soon saw Aloe erinacea, growing with plants almost in rows and on top of each other—as we did at Rosh Pinah in South-West Africa. We drove on to find Aloe kamisensis, tall fine plants but, as seems usual here, only just a few of them in any one place. All day we were to see the odd Conophytum, still with its skin on, and often out in the open in the blazing sun. Nearby there were Crassula unicornis (a tall type) and quite close, searching for shade, I found a Cotyledon, a Kalanchoë, an Euphorbia and Cheiridopsis—all under one bush of Namaqualand daisy.

There were a lot of different species of Pelargoniums, all completely black, though one plant even had a brave little yellow flower. Occasionally we saw a Kalanchoë with its blue-green leaves in flower, but the Cotyledons were all black and parched. The Euphorbias here are thicker-stemmed and more like a Kleinia, and we found one black-looking Stapelia variegata with tiny flowers braving the heat. Here also was a Caralluma, rather tall and quite black.

Helpers from the Nature Reserve collecting a large Aloe for the Museum

The last phase of our outward journey took us to see the Pachypodium namaquensis, the 'Half Man' as they call them. We had four miles to go along a river bed—and what a river bed it was. Even I went up and down like a pea on a plate. Suddenly we turned out of the valley up a steep track made mostly of broken rock and stones. It was not very long—just some four hundred yards—and before we came to the end there was the most perilous turn, very steep, just wide enough for the Land-Rover, above a sheer drop to perdition. To make it worse, it was so steep that you could not see the road in front, in order to judge where your wheels were. But all went well, and we came to the Pachypodiums—again not many of them, possibly some twenty or thirty. All were brown-ribbed, tapering to the top and full of thorns. Some were eight or ten feet high, and always had their heads with a green tip, tilted towards the north. It was

very exciting to see Mr Dumoulay and the boys dig one up. It was about five feet high and they had a hard fight, but as they had all the right tools they got it out with its root intact, to take back to their garden in the reserve.

Nearby they found some five-headed Anacampseros and a few tiny Haworthias. Soon the road improved a bit, so that we took two and a half hours to do sixteen miles! We passed some fine Euphorbias—a clump type of plant with twenty to thirty stems branching from ground level up to a height of eight or ten feet. They seemed in excellent condition. Nearby were the odd Hoodia Bainii (up to three feet high) looking pretty sick. Our last plant was one solitary Aloe garipensis—bright red and about two feet high—sitting proudly between and on top of two great boulders; and there it remained, as the team just could not move the boulders without damaging the roots.

A fine Pachypodium Namaquensis

The Curator of the Nature Reserve at Springbok with a Pachypodium Namaquensis

Aloe melanocentra growing in the Van Heerdens' interesting cactus garden in Springbok

In their natural habitat

5 South Africa in springtime

I had always wanted to see the spring flowers for which South Africa is justly famous—both the succulent plants in which I had been interested for years, and the wild flowers, which are very beautiful when they bloom. The rains had been very good in the winter (July–August) and early spring (September) which was lucky, as when there is only a small rainfall there may be a year without spring flowers and this can happen for several years on end. I planned to arrive in mid-September and to be there till the middle of October. This gave a useful bracket in time, as in certain areas like the Karoo garden at Worcester, the succulents come into flower several weeks later than the Namaqualand daisies and Gazanias in Namaqualand. The weather was beginning to warm up after the winter, but they were not as yet using the swimming pool at the hotel. I hired an excellent Ford Capri and started to plan my journeys in accordance with the latest available information on the state of the flowers in each particular area. The flowers in Namaqualand were reaching their peak, so I set out at once for Springbok, the capital town of Namaqualand. On the way up we arranged to see the succulents round Vredendal. So we broke our journey at Van Rhynsdorp. It was too cold to sit out of doors—and my party slept with several blankets and an electric fire on.

There were some patches of lovely colour and everywhere the countryside was green. I had seen Cotyledons and Euphorbias in January, when they looked dead or dying in the brown, parched waste—and you did not feel that any of them would live, let alone flower again. A few had not survived, but the great majority were looking healthy and strong. It is wonderful to see what the rains can do. I went over to Vredendal to see Harry Hall, whom I had not seen since he left the National Botanical Gardens at Kirstenbosch, where for many years he had looked after the succulents. His wife was a botanist, and her father lived in Vredendal —we at once recognised his house because Harry Hall had planted a fine display of South African succulents in the garden. For some years he had been the Nationalist member of parliament. He had fought on the Boer side in the South African War and when I went into his house he gave me a great soldier's welcome, and brought out all his photos and medals for me to see.

He owned a large track of ground, mostly arid and stony sheep farming land, and Harry Hall took us out on to it and showed us many interesting varieties of succulents growing in this wild hill country. There was a tiny Conophytum and Argyroderma Hallii discovered and named by Harry Hall himself. I saw for the first time the tiny brown Oophytum nordenstansii, sometimes with a white flower larger than itself. There were Dactylopsis and Monilaria brevifolia, with its attractive white flower, and occasionally, when we came across Hymenocyclys purpureo-croceus, we were reminded of the purple heather in Scotland.

We continued our journey up the fine new tarmac road, which is now completed all the way to

Oophytum Nordenstamsii on the stony hillsides near Vredental

Dactylopsis on the arid slopes near Vredental

Springbok, with the colour growing in intensity as we drove farther north. Round Garies, in particular, we saw vast patches of yellow and blue, and in one area close to the old road, Frances Denby in my party found over twenty varieties of wild flowers, the hybridized versions of which I have in my gardens in England. We were lucky to get some good photographs and to find a place for a picnic, with flowers all round us, because some days later the flies here were so persistent that it was impossible even to get out of the car. They seemed to tear along the road behind in a great black swarm and to launch a massed attack on us directly we stopped.

The wild flowers round Springbok do not really open until the sun comes up, and it was no use starting out too early, but it was interesting to get into the area we had chosen for the day in time to sit there and await the visible opening of the flowers, the whole vista gradually turning into one glorious golden or scarlet carpet. The colours of the flowers and the green foliage were glorious, especially perhaps to those of us who had only been to Namaqualand once before, and that in January, when the entire countryside was brown, and all the plants looked as if they were already dead or about to die. The Mesembryanthymum and Namaqualand daisy bushes had been black, and even with the most vivid imagination, it had been difficult to realise that one day, if only the rains

Monilaria Brevifolia in flower on the barren slopes near Vredental

Wild flowers in bloom near Concordia

Wild flowers in full bloom on the old Garies Road near Springbok

came, the countryside would turn into the glorious riot of flowers we were now able to see.

We were told that the best display of colour was on some farms at Concordia only a few miles from Springbok. We motored out there, the last few miles between massifs of vast rocks—it was a fantastic approach. We got to the gateway into the farm to which we were going in plenty of time to see the flowers start to open. It was a lovely day with clear blue sky and sunshine, and warming up. We drove along a track for a few hundred yards. At first the colours were rather faint and disappointing and it all seemed rather dull. And then as you watched them the flowers began to open— minute by minute the colours became more intense.

We were in a splendid position, on a small hillock where we could see for two or three miles. Gradually we watched the most breathtaking transformation as the whole countryside around us and for miles ahead of us became one glorious carpet of gold and scarlet glistening in the morning sun behind us, making the picture more vivid and wonderful for us. It was a glorious amphitheatre ringed by mountains, a fitting framework in which to see this spectacle, with small rocky outcrops, often surmounted by a fine tall Aloe dichotoma standing like a sentry, protecting guardsmen on parade.

We motored some miles to several different vantage points. Sometimes the colours were scarlet, sometimes gold, but everywhere it was a wonderful

The author on a carpet of Namaqualand Daisies and Gazanias at Concordia

Aloes growing at Optenhorst near Wellington

A fine specimen of Aloe Dichotoma on the cliffs around Concordia

93

sight. We did not see as many different plants as we had done down at Garies, and there were very few succulents but, as a display this was superb. We went up too, to some of the rocky outcrops leading up to the mountain passes, and here in the cliff sides and often in the midst of tangled rocks we found a larger variety of individual plants. I was to see other lovely displays of wild flowers going up and down to Namaqualand but nothing to compare in its intensity to the maximum concentration at Concordia.

We motored back to Cape Town, and my next tour was to the Little Karoo, where Professor Rycroft, director of the National Botanical Gardens at Kirstenbosch, told me that I would be going just at the right time, as the flowers there normally bloom later than they do in Namaqualand. The Little Karoo is a fascinating area for succulents and it contains an astonishing variety of interesting plants in a comparatively small area. It starts about a hundred miles north of Cape Town, and there is a lovely drive over the Klein Drakenstein mountains to get there.

The road from Cape Town to the Little Karoo via Worcester and Montague leads out along the low lying country behind Table Mountain. On the left of the road rise the Twin Pearls of Paarl, and the Du Toit Pass lies ahead. It is a magnificent road built by Italian prisoners of war in World War II, with steady gradients stretching for at least twelve miles to the summit of the pass, where there were many Protea bushes, a riot of orange and red colours when in full flower. Protea cynaroides, which bears the largest flower of all the Protea (sometimes six to ten inches across) is the national emblem of South Africa, and enjoys the damp atmosphere of the clouds which so often girdle the summit. In winter they stand up to snow and frost, but one must remember that the frost is usually followed by a bright, sunny day. Quite close to the Protea, and hanging over the rocks, we saw a magnificent great bush of Oscularia deltoides, at least six feet square, with a glorious sheen of greeny-blue. There was a wonderful view back over Paarl towards Cape Town, a horizon full of vineyards above the township. Northwards, too, there was a fine view away over the Klein Drakenstein with its gaunt peaks and mauve-coloured hills, and as we looked into the distance it was easy to realize the extent of this great range, which prevents the rain-bearing winds from the Atlantic penetrating to the arid regions of the Little Karoo.

The road ran on down the Hex river to Worcester, where we went to the Karoo Gardens with their indefatigable curator, Mr Stamer. As we approached the Gardens, which have ample water laid on, we saw on our right a glorious little Kopje, which was a blaze of colour—predominantly the scarlet Drosanthemum speciosum. On the Kopjes around the house there were Lampranthus speciosum, with its red, orange and pink flowers and mauve and purple Ruschias mingled with red and orange Gazanias whilst on all sides were Aloe striata, Aloe ferox and Euphorbia ingens all in flower. There were many Euphorbias, including a magnificent Euphorbia horrida and some Euphorbia coerulescens which the farmers scorch and grind as food for their cattle. In fact, on all sides, it was an African treasury of Aloes and Euphorbias. As we stood on the top of the Kopje by the curator's house, there was a glorious view across the flowering Kopje over the plain to the attractive town of Worcester with its white-walled houses. From here we started our tour to the beds on the slopes at the back of the house. We saw many kinds of Lithops, which are very easy to study here, as they are laid out in groups and covered with small white pebbles. There were, too, Anacampseros, Cheiridopsis, Haworthia truncata, Pleiospilos and Muiria Hortenseae. Lower down the slope, planted in the shade of the shaly rocks, there were Stapelias, Huernias, Carallumas, Haworthias and other shade-loving plants, cunningly sited to get the maximum sun in the winter afternoon, and also in such a manner as to keep their roots cool and to avoid the fierce rays of the midday sun.

We drove on through Worcester, and on the way to Montague we found the roadside gay with red, orange and yellow flowers of Gazanias, with a background of mauve and purple Mesembryanthemums. On our way we saw a lot of sheep and goats, and we were told that, in the main, succulents are not devoured because stock does not like them and that even on farms where there is the scantiest of natural grazing one often sees fat juicy, Gibbaeums, Glottiphyllums and Vanheerdias quite ignored, whereas the wiry, woody shrubs such as Eberlanzias and Ruschias are eaten down. Probably ninety per cent of the food of the sheep is composed of these plants, since grass as we in Europe and America know it will not grow. It is a well-known fact that the finest quality wool comes from the vast farms where Eberlanzia spinosa and other spiny forms of Ruschias are the prevalent vegetation.

There is another view that only when the animals are suffering from thirst will they have a go at an old Aloe variegata or Glottiphyllum. There are, however, some genera they do seem to seek out, especially Haworthia, goats being the chief offenders. Sometimes they will even seek out some species and ignore others. For instance, it has been known for every plant of Glottiphyllum arrectum to be nibbled severely, whilst the nearby Glottiphyllum fragrans was untouched. In Calitzdorp on the Ceres Karoo there are hundreds of the beautiful Glottiphyllum regium growing almost to the exclusion of all else within a few yards of a village teeming with goats, but they show barely any signs of damage, except from the hooves of the goats.

The rare Muiria Hortenseae growing on its usual white, shaley patch

A magnificent Euphorbia Caput Medusae in flower

Euphorbia Susannae, a tiny plant with a long tap root, growing amid Gibbaeums

Some lovely Aloes in flower by the roadside near Montague

On bare patches amongst the scattered houses are enormous clumps of the giant form of Gibbaeum heathii and masses of Carpobrotus, Hymenocyclus and Cephalophyllums, all similarly ignored. It is known that Dinteranthus has been pawed from the ground in times of drought in Bushmanland, although only the tips of the leaves and the thin dry roots have been devoured. Since the animals could have nibbled the leaves without the effort of pawing, did they really prefer the roots?

In parts of the eastern Cape, where Euphorbia cœrulescens and Euphorbia ledienii grow by the square mile, they are cut for cattle fodder. Farmers depend a great deal on this food, but to anyone coming straight from England it is a strange sight, even when one has read about it before.

Just beyond Robertson there was a sandy-looking patch which looked as if it had had a bulldozer working on it, and here it is possible to find Pectinaria breviloba, a member of the Stapelia family, growing in soft sand under bushes, with its long white stems deep underground. It is a difficult plant to cultivate as its roots are very scanty, and most probably its white stems absorb nourishment underground as freely as its true roots.

Some way beyond Robertson, the road passes through a gorge between the hills known as Kogmans Kloof, its steep sides showing vertical rock strata such as one seldom sees. On the lower slopes there was a reddish-brown sandstone with the same typical warm colouring as is found in Karoo Poort on the Ceres Karoo, and much erosion everywhere. In many places there were Aloes and Kalanchoes clinging precariously to the sides of the cliffs. On emerging from the gorge the attractive little town of Montague appears, almost surrounded by towering mountains, and to the east of the town the Little Karoo proper commences. It is countryside which changes almost hourly in its variety, interest and degree of vegetation. At first the country was green and covered with Rhenoster bushes, with the Gazanias and brightly-coloured Mesembryanthemums showing up everywhere, like a drive through one, long, gaily-coloured garden. There were hills on either side of the road, mostly flat-topped, and sometimes covered with purple Ruschia and scarlet Drosanthemum speciosum. Away on the right lie the Langeberg chain of mountains, a hazy mauve in the distance with their weird and scraggy mountain tops more often than not merged with a long blanket of cloud.

At first where there is a good water supply, the vegetation was lush with fields of corn, but as you get father on to the Karoo the vegetation dwindles, though the colour may still persist. When the first spring flowers are out, you may suddenly, as we did, stand spellbound in front of some Kopje which is just one blaze of wondrous colours, succulents at their very best. 'Our' Kopje was a small narrow knife-edge feature of russet-coloured

A lovely clump of the purple Ruschia which covers miles of the Karoo

Drosanthemum speciosum blooms in the spring and covers miles of the Karoo with scarlet flowers

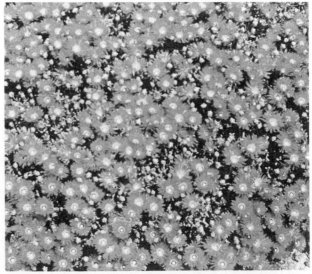

A magnificent great clump of the scarlet Drosanthemum speciosum

A glorious view of Mesembryanthemums
and wild flowers in bloom over the Karoo
to the mountains beyond

A lovely little kopje in the Karoo, gay with
the red Drosanthemum speciosum and other
succulents and wild flowers

97

shale, its rocks piled up in fantastic strata, as if the higher ones were balanced in mid-air.

The first plant to catch one's eye was Drosanthemum speciosum, a glorious flower, sometimes scarlet and sometimes of various orange hues. The predominant colour, however, came from the purple Ruschia karroica, and there were patches of white Aridaria splendens and yellow Hymenocyclus luteus. It was just as if one had suddenly arrived at a beautifully-planted rock garden, but nature seemed to have blended her colours and arranged her flowers just that much better than man would do. It gave one an idea of how fine a succulent garden could be made in those parts of Africa where Mesembryanthemums will flourish. On the outskirts of the Karoo, where the rainfall is a little higher than on the Karoo proper, there were glorious colours everywhere. There were miles and miles of purple Ruschia and Lampranthus Haworthii with a glorious mauve sheen, stretching as far as the eye can see and giving a colour effect

rather mindful of the Jacaranda trees in full bloom in Pretoria. By the roadside there were gaily-coloured little patches of orange and red Gazanias while in every direction were splashes of red, yellow and white to lighten up the purple fields. Wherever there was reasonable soil, there were fields of Mesembryanthemums in flower, but we were told, however that in a few more weeks the horizon would have gone back to one, long, grey-green vista of Rhenoster Bush.

The 'vygies', as they call them, give the signal that spring has come to the Karoo, for when they cover the veldt in September the gaily-coloured landscape of the desert mounts in grandeur day after day. As we motored through the townships of the Karoo we passed unexpectedly beautiful gardens, often as in Montague, with lovely red and mauve Bougainvillea growing alongside Aloes in flower, whilst the multi-coloured Mesembryanthemums vie with the roses and the beautiful red flowers of Erythrina caffra, which appear before

A magnificent Aloe spinosissima with profuse red flowers

A fine Aloe hybrid with red and yellow flower spikes

Aloe striata with some glorious flowerheads in the Karoo Succulent Garden at Worcester

the leaves. Its common name is 'Kaffirboom' and it is one of the finest flowering trees in the world. It is frequently planted as a street tree. In Paarl, it can be seen interplanted with the Jacaranda with its mauve-blue flowers. In some gardens there were large trees of the American Cereus Spachianus, which looked very healthy and are glorious when in flower.

Not far from Montague there were banks of Aloe mitriformis, which have lovely russet red leaves, and which, as they grow older, fall flat on the ground like Aloe distans. Nearby was Haworthia margaritifera, a native of Worcester, which sometimes has a branching flower spike two feet high, and is similar to those smaller ones which grow near Cape Agulhas.

In the same neighbourhood there was Adromischus maculatus, no longer red and scarlet as on the Cereus Karoo, but growing a dark green colour under bushes. Close by was Sutherlandia frutescens, a leguminous shrub, with its scarlet flowers and almost transparent inflated fruit, and often Aptosimum depressum, the Karoo violet, with its attractive little bluish-mauve flower with white markings. Mingling among these plants were many interesting specimens, amongst others Pelargonium crispum with crinkly, lemon-scented leaves and pink and white flowers and Adromischus leucophyllus growing in rock fissures with its white leaves and Crassula expansa.

At the end of the day, when darkness descends, and you can no longer look on this garden treasury, there is no need to drive out of the Karoo again, as a very comfortable night can be spent in the excellent hotels in Montague. The Little Karoo was a fitting conclusion to a wonderful month in the South African spring. We were lucky to have struck a year when there had been such good rains, and luckier still to have made many good friends who had helped us to choose a programme in which we managed to reach each area just when the flowers were at their best.

Namaqualand Daisies and Gazanias in full bloom at Concordia near Springbok

Conophytum petraeum growing on a hillside under the shade of a rock. Another plant growing nearby in full sun was bright red

Succulents all over the world

Most people think that the succulent plants in which we are interested come only from America and South Africa; and it is certainly true to say that the entire family Cactaceae, with the exception perhaps of some species of Rhipsalis, come from the New World. It is equally true to say that, although the majority of succulents come from Southern Africa, quite a number hail from other parts of Africa and from many other parts of the globe, almost from Pole to Pole. It is, however, mostly the American and African plants which have been imported by collectors and have been propagated and put into circulation in Europe by nurserymen. For this reason, American and African plants are much better known to us than plants with similar characteristics that grow in other parts of the world. These other genera are very interesting, partly because they are rare in cultivation and partly because we know little about them.

As I have said, some people imagine that succulent plants thrive only in deserts, whilst others conjure up visions of all deserts as vast sandy regions devoid of all plant life. In actual fact, as we know, neither of these descriptions is strictly accurate. The vast majority of succulent plants live in the prairie or karoo country, on the edges of the deserts proper. In real deserts, such as the Sahara, the Australian sand plains and the Gobi, little vegetation exists. Deserts are situated in regions where there is plenty of sunshine and warmth, but where rainfall and water supply are intermittent and where rainstorms are few and far between. It follows that the plants indigenous to these parts must be drought-resistant. What few of us realize is that the conditions of vegetable life in high mountains can be very similar to these desert conditions. In the higher mountain regions, where there is a rapid drainage of water and scarcity of soil, precipitation is much less than on the slopes. The continual winds in the rarified mountain atmosphere dry up everything very quickly; and the plants themselves are sometimes in ground which is frozen and are therefore physiologically dry. It is for these reasons that certain plants living on high mountains are equipped to withstand drought. Sedums, Sempervivums and other dwarf rosette plants are typical examples to be found in the high Alps and the Caucasus, whilst Poyas and Dychias come from the Andes, and Sedums flourish in the Himalayas and in the mountains of Japan and in China which are especially rich in them. There are Sedums, too, throughout Europe and even as far afield as Greenland, and they include many colourful annual species, amongst which is the attractive Sedum coeruleum, which brings to Europe the fame of being the only continent to possess a blue-flowered succulent.

The Mediterranean

There are many succulents round the Mediterranean coastlines of France, Spain, Italy and the Balkans, mostly Agaves, Aloes and Euphorbias. They were imported from America and Africa, traditionally in ballast by Columbus' sailors, but now they have become naturalized in their new homes. You sometimes find them growing wild on the hillsides, though they are mostly in cultivated gardens or are specially planted to stop erosion, like those along railway and other embankments. The most attractive Aloe vera which is often used for medicinal purposes, is a native of the Mediterranean region, Sempervivums also flourish, especially in Spain and Portugal. Opuntias are sometimes used as hedges, as in Spain, and in Israel they use Opuntia hedges as part of their frontier defences in areas which would otherwise be indefensible.

One of the best-known collections is to be found in the Jardin Exotique on the cliff sides which drop down sheer to the sea in Monaco. It is a wonderful position as it is protected from the cold winds and is normally free from frost, though in the bad winter of 1956, when there was continuous frost for several weeks, a lot of plants were damaged. The gardens were started in the middle of the nineteenth century under the patronage of Prince Albert I, who arranged for a well-known architect and engineer, Louis Notari, to lay out what were first known as the 'Hanging Gardens'. It was a brilliant design on the sheer rock face. Augustin Gastand then planted the garden and his original layout has been the basis of the plan ever since. There is a broad pathway, several hundred yards in length, which descends in a gentle zigzag slope down the cliff, sometimes crossing narrow gullies on attractive bridges and occasionally with small balconies from which you can look over the sea cliffs. Throughout the walk there are hundreds of magnificent cactus and succulent plants on all sides. There are large clumps of Aloes, which are particularly lovely in the spring with their golden and red spikes, while tall Cereus and vast Prickly Pear Opuntias stand by the side of a bridge over a gully. The pathway leads on through a vertitable forest of Cereus peruvianus. There is a fine view over the Palace of Monaco with Agaves and Opuntias in the foreground, whilst a little farther on you look back towards the mountains from a tiny plateau lined with Yuccas and Agaves. The path crosses a small ravine, where there are clumps of giant Echinocactus Grusonii mingled with Euphorbia splendens, and huge banks of shrubby Mesembryanthemums, which are a blaze of mauve and red in the spring. Then you can see a magnificent great plant of Euphorbia clandestina with heads spreading out all round, while through another clump of Opuntias there are glorious views down to the town and harbour. Finally,

**Agave Americana variegata against a
background of the cathedral of Palma de
Mallorca**

**Two views looking over Monaco to the
Mediterranean, with Cereus and Aloes
growing high up on the cliffside of the famous
Jardin Exotique**

as you look behind you, there are Cleistocactus Strausii and Trichocereus standing gaunt against the clear blue sky. It is indeed a Mexican wonderland planted on a cliff-side above the Mediterranean, with all the beauty of Monte Carlo below.

In the south of France there are many Prickly Pears, Euphorbias and Agaves and it is the same along the Mediterranean coast of Spain. About fifty miles from Barcelona on the rugged Costa Brava coast you will find at Blanes the Jardin d'Acclimatacion called 'Pinya de Rosa' – which was laid out in large irregular beds, edged by rocks and stones, with stone plants zigzagging everywhere between the beds. Marble steps flanked by ornamental urns lead down to this exhaustive collection of Opuntias, and away beyond is the Spanish house with a vista through the trees down to the blue sea. Here are the lovely blue spineless Opuntia crassa, whose red fruit is curiously enough covered with spines; and some fine specimens of the long tongue-leaved Opuntia linguiformia. There is a large bed with every kind of Opuntia microdasys, great spreading bushes such as you seldom see, including Opuntia pallida, which is not often found in England, and which was in bloom with a yellow flower in September.

Beyond the Opuntias, the ground drops away towards the sea and there is a punch-bowl with beds full of Mesembryanthemums which are a wonderful spectacle when they are in flower in the spring. Below the Opuntias are the Aloes, whilst above them are the Agaves. The Aloes and Mesembryanthemums were badly damaged in the 1956 frosts and the large Opuntias were reduced to grim-looking stems; but even a few months after the frosts new green pads were shooting up everywhere from ground level. The Agaves are tougher and did not suffer so much. There are some fine Agave Americana variegata and a particularly lovely blue Agave winteriana.

There is also an interesting collection of smaller plants, some of which are in heated houses. I was thrilled to see some very good Stapelias growing on a terrace wall in pans, each plant between two large geraniums in pots to give it shade. The rare Diplocyatha ciliata of the Stapelia group with a lovely light-green flower was amongst others in flower in September. Below this terrace is a really fine collection of Lithops, Conophytums and other small Mesembryanthemums, laid out with small rocks on a large staging some three and a half feet wide. Each plant is very well labelled and it gives the effect that they are growing naturally, though they are in fact grouped very carefully by genera.

In Majorca you mostly see the Prickly Pear, which by this time has become almost indigenous. I saw one particularly interesting field of Prickly Pear – cropped out in straight rows. I arrived just at the right time as the trees were filled with maroon

coloured fruit, like plum trees in full crop. A man was coming round them taking off the fruit quickly and accurately with long wooden tongs, with which he placed them in baskets on the ground.

In Italy there are succulents on the Mediterranean coast and at an acute bend along the Corniche road on the Italian Riviera, between San Remo and Bordighera, you will see stretching high above you a small corner of the Mexican desert, belonging to an Italian nurseryman. It is built like an Italian vineyard on a series of dry wall terraces rising high above the road. It is a steep climb, and in front of the cliff-side wall on every terrace there is a background of tall Cereus, predominantly white in colour. Fine specimens, six feet tall and eight inches in diameter, of Cephalocereus senilis and slender white plants of Cleistocactus Strausii stand out, with a light-green Euphorbia candelabra variety Erytrea, against the sombre columns of Cereus peruvianus monstrosus. Then there are some large Cephalocereus Palmeri, with white hairs on green bodies, and in the distance are lovely white-haired Espostoa lanata standing alongside Cleistocactus jujuyensis. There are some particularly fine clumps of Trichocereus strigosus with masses of white trumpet-shaped flowers if you happen to be there in the summer, and farther on there is a magnificent group of great golden Echinocactus Grusonii. All around, too, are many interesting smaller plants including Opuntia microdasys albispina and a host of fine Astrophytum myriostigma and ornatum.

A collection of cacti, including Opuntias and Epiphytes, growing outside a house on Ibiza, and (bottom) a fine display of Cereus, Agaves and Opuntias at Puerta de la Cruz, Tenerife, Canary Islands

104

Opuntia flowers, with a bumble bee as guest

**Picking the 'Prickly Pear' fruit from
Opuntias, using the wooden tongs customary
on Mallorca**

Canary Islands

You will also find succulents here, particularly Aeoniums, Euphorbias, Prickly Pears and Agaves. On the small island of Lanzarotte I have seen large areas black with hills and ravines of lava, where Prickly Pear and Euphorbias are sometimes found growing on some small patch of clean ground. They certainly brighten up the volcanic scene. You can motor right up to the top of one of the lava-covered volcanoes, and here they use the hot springs bubbling out of the mountain to cook their food. On the lower parts of the island there are big areas covered with Prickly Pear, which have been planted out for the fruit, and to give these colour there are some Euphorbia trees with a yellow flower.

The British Isles

There are a few indigenous Sedums and only one Cotyledon, now renamed Umbilicus. Generally speaking, the cacti and succulents which we find in England today are not indigenous and most of them are kept throughout the winter in greenhouses or in private houses. It is different in the Scilly Islands, where you find a magnificent succulent garden in Tresco Abbey Gardens.

On Tresco, which is about two miles from St. Mary's and which you reach by motor boat, there are more trees than on the other islands.

They were planted by the first member of the present Dorrien-Smith family to come to Tresco about 1840; but the winds were so strong that in the first thirty-two years the trees only grew some twelve feet. The Smiths, however, were undeterred. They searched for specimens that would stand up to these conditions and, at the same time, for flowering ones that would enhance the beauty of the islands.

Within the shelter of these trees and quite close to Tresco Abbey you will find the best outdoor succulent garden in Great Britain. The plants are growing in a light, friable, well-drained soil with plenty of additional humus from the trees which have been planted on the island. Even those plants which are perched precariously on walls and banks, seemingly with no soil, look strong and healthy. It is indeed an ideal soil and climate for them, but their chief enemy is the wind.

The garden consists of some six acres and it is long and narrow, rising some fifty feet on one side, and surrounded on all sides by trees. The succulents are mostly from Africa and the Canary Islands, though there are a variety of fine Agaves, including an Agave salmiana which is one of the largest I have ever seen, almost twelve feet across. It was a splendid sight in the sun with golden Gazanias on the bank below it. As you leave the Abbey by the top path there is a fine cluster of

Succulents flowering amid the lava on Lanzarote Island

Euphorbias in flower on Lanzarote

An Opuntia (Prickly Pear) fruit farm in the Canary Islands

Aloe brevifolia, with at least a hundred small heads, crimson red in colour nestling in crevices in the rockside. On all sides there are Aeoniums including Aeonium tabulaeforme, Aeonium Canariensis, Aeonium cuneatum and Aeonium nobile with its red flower, growing happily on the sides of rock faces, walls and buildings. In June, many of them were in flower with their golden spines often high in the air. On all sides, with their tall blue flower spikes silhouetted against the clear blue sky were the giant Echiums, and close to them were Puya chilensis with their tall yellow flower heads and Puya bertoraniana with its lovely green blue flower on tall slender flower spikes. Everywhere there are gaily coloured Mesembryanthemums, in many shades of red, pink and purple, often merged in a mass of colour with multi-coloured Pelargoniums. (There is one particularly lovely apricot pink, one hybridized under the name of Tresco apricot.)

There is a fine display of Aloes many of which flower in rotation from January onwards including some attractive small Aloes aristata with attractive little yellow and red flower heads. Amongst others we saw Aloe vera, a lovely beige colour, Aloe gracilis, Aloe ferox and Aloe microcantha.

East Africa

In Kenya you can see some magnificent tall Candelabra Euphorbias fully forty feet high and rivalling in height and majesty the giant branched Cerei, such as the Saguaros in Arizona and the Pringlei in Mexico. You also find there some magnificent bushes of Kalanchoë beharensis with their large ungainly leaves, sometimes ten or twelve feet high.

Seed-pods of Euphorbia

A vast Euphorbia candelabra near Nairobi

It was the imagination and gardening genius of the (now retired) Parks Superintendent, Mr Greensmith, that has made Nairobi the most beautiful city in the world. He raised some twenty different species of Bougainvillia, in almost every tint of red, pink, and orange. There is a fine road system in and around the city and he planted these up with hedges of Bougainvillia. The traffic islands became a riot of colour, with a background of large Euphorbias, Agaves and Prickly Pears. In the city itself, he made some lovely standards by grafting on to long stems bush trees of Bougainvillia, Hibiscus and other flowering shrubs. He was much encouraged by President Kenyatta who enjoyed the beauty in the streets and realised its value as a tourist attraction. Mr Greensmith's garden was in keeping with the excellent floral layout of the municipal grounds and roadways of the city, and was well worth a visit. The setting is charming with fine trees, some covered to their tops with red and mauve Bougainvillia, around a beautifully kept lawn, which is broken up by ornamental streams, banks of flowering shrubs and beds of annuals. All manner of succulent plants are planted alongside these trees and flowering shrubs, and also in the many flower beds with the smaller plants.

Euphorbia splendens see page 63

A tall Euphorbia ingens in the garden of the Park Superintendent in Nairobi

A vast Euphorbia in the garden of the Park Superintendent

Near the house there is an imposing group of Euphorbias quite forty feet high, whilst not so far from them you will see tall Cereus spachianus from America, doing equally well, alongside a bed of scarlet Poinsettias. In one place there is a particularly fine plant of Opuntia monacantha variegata with its highly decorative pads, while close by there is a magnificent specimen of Kalanchoë beharensis, with its great soft leaves shaped like an elephant's ear. At the feet of these monsters are beds of succulents, including masses of Sedum Adolphii, whose sandy colour blends so well with the gay colours of the annuals. There are several interesting Kalanchoës from Madagascar, many Sedums and Crassulas and even a few cacti such as Echinopsis and Chamaecereus silvestrii. There are groups of Euphorbia spendens, including the yellow variety, Euphorbia Hislopii with its tiny red flower, and a ten foot high Adenium.

Madagascar

The individuality of the flora and fauna suggest that this island has existed as a separate land mass for an extraordinarily long period of time. Some of the life forms have African or Indian affinities but so many curious modifications and organisms of type occur, which you seem to find nowhere else, that it is hard to resist thinking of a 'lost world'. Prehistoric hangovers include the now extinct but late-surviving Aephyorhis, a bird which laid the largest eggs of all. Madagascar is a high rainfall area with tropical forest conditions in the coastal areas—higher up it is colder and ice forms on the mountains. In general, however, Madagascan succulents such as Euphorbia splendens (the Crown of Thorns), with its little scarlet and sometimes yellow flowers, required higher winter temperature.

Unfortunately I could only go there during the rainy season, and being without a Land Rover I could not go to the most interesting areas, where the communications are primitive and difficult. During my stay, I flew down to Nossi Bé, a most attractive resort, where it poured in torrents all the time for three days and nights. We flew from Johannesburg to Tananarive, a rambling town on a series of hills, with attractive houses with wooden balconies. Here are a gay, laughing people, still very much influenced by the French. We went out six miles to the Tsimbazaza Botanical Gardens, where curiously enough only a rather small section showed indigenous plants from Madagascar. We did however find many Euphorbias, and a selection of Adenias, Didieras, Alluaudias and Pachypodiums.

From Tulear I motored round the countryside in a two-wheel-drive taxi, seeing about ten species of Euphorbias, including some tall trees with yellow flowers. I also saw a lot of Didieras, many of them tall and thin and very much branched with tiny green leaves and spines all up the main stem and the branches.

Tree Euphorbia near Tulear

A fine Euphorbia Stencoloda near Tulear

Alluaudia in the Botanical Gardens of Tananarive

A close-up of the long, thin branches of a Didiera in Madagascar

Pachypodium at Tulear

Pachypodium in flower at Tulear

A well-shaped, tall Didiera growing among Euphorbias near Tulear, Madagascar

Aden

At the other side of the Red Sea, we find Adeniums in Arabia growing under conditions similar to those in South Africa, together with Cotyledons and Huernias. We went to Aden, where we took a local aeroplane up to Mukerias, some 100 miles from Aden. I was on my way to stay with Major Simon Beck, who was at that time the political agent and the intelligence officer on the Yemeni frontier. It was an exciting flight in a plane full of local Arabs with their sheep, goats and chickens on the seats. After stopping at an air-strip close under the 10,000-foot escarpment, we had to fly to the top of it by zig-zagging along the face of the cliffs until we had reached the air strip at the top. I found the political agent in a small fortified house, with a mortar mounted on top, with which they used to repel the constant night attacks made on them. We went out to look for succulents close to the house, and we were always escorted by three or four local scouts armed to the teeth and also carrying a spade to help us dig up the plants.

In about an hour we found fifteen different kinds of succulents, all pink and maroon in colour from lack of water, mostly Aloes, Huernias and Cotyledons. By the political agent's house there was a splendid great Euphorbia with a lovely maroon flower. We motored out over the country consisting of black volcanic rocks without any form of vegetation, always accompanied by a truckload of soldiers, as we looked down over the Yemeni border.

Euphorbia in flower—a glorious sight at the Political Agent's house in Mukeirias

A very parched Aloe still growing strongly in the arid, stony ground near Mukeirias, South Arabia

**Cereus and other Cacti struggling to exist in
the disease-ridden, evil 'hotland' near Coro
in Venezuela**

Aloe garipensis looking very burnt-up amidst the rocks

Euphorbias flourishing on the arid stony ground at Mukeirias

The author digging up succulents with two armed guards at Mukeirias

A Stapelia in inhospitable stony ground near Mukeirias

Australia

In Australia and New Zealand there are practically no native succulents except for Carpobrotus and Ceropegias, but Opuntias were imported into Australia and have become naturalized. They were brought in to provide a cheap and safe hedge before the days of barbed wire. Opuntia inermis, which originally came from the tropical areas of America, was among them. A free and strong grower in its own country, it settled down at once in Australia and pads which fell from the plants propagated freely, so that within a comparatively short time huge stretches of country became covered with Opuntias, and became in parts impenetrable to man or beast. Something had to be done to check this invasion and, after considerable research by the best scientists in Australia, a moth by the name of Cactoblastis cactorum has been brought into action. It has lived up to its Latin name and it has veritably blasted the cacti out of the Australian Bush. Its means of attack is to lay its eggs on the spines of the Opuntias. In due course the eggs hatch out and the caterpillars burrow into the pads and stems of the plants. As they advance, they eat away the plant tissue until eventually it is reduced to a gaunt skeleton and collapses.

Trinidad

I first went out to Trinidad in the West Indies in time to see the first test match of Colin Cowdrey's team. I had an introduction to an orchid collector, and I wrote and asked him if he could show me any cacti growing in the wild. He replied that he would be delighted to do so, if we could spare a day from the test match. I soon found that we were going out in a motor launch to a chain of islands between Trinidad and Venezuela. After what I had seen some years ago on the island off Guaymas, I was not surprised to see the tall stems of Cereus on the banks of the islands, though they were growing under quite different conditions from those in Mexico. There was heavy undergrowth everywhere, so that if you had wanted to 'browse' amongst the cacti, as you could do in Mexico, you would have had to cut your way through the bush with a hatchet.

We got ashore in a few places and found a dark green Agave, a few Opuntias vulgaris and a lot of Epiphytes of the hylocereus and selenicereus type. The tallest Cereus were usually only some ten feet high and with narrowish stems, sometimes fanning out some three feet up the trunk like the spokes of an umbrella.

Jamaica

I arrived at Kingston airport for the test match. After the match, in which, incidentally, we were gassed during the bottle-throwing and subsequent riot, when the tear-gas blew back over the VIP's stands, we motored through Spanish Town over

Cereus growing in the spray on the shore of an island off Trinidad

the hills to Runaway Bay. A great deal of the countryside is tropical and we saw a lot of Orchids and Epiphytes high up in the trees. We took the road to Ochorios in order to drive through the famous Fern Gully, an eerie place lined with the most gigantic bamboos and every kind of palm tree and fern you can think of.

While we were up in the Runaway Bay and Montego Bay area, we took our car into the smaller roads in the hills to explore the very lovely countryside. Everywhere we saw a mauvy-pink flowering Bryophyllum and the occasional Aloe vera, both of which (the latter for medicinal purposes) must have been brought into Jamaica by the slaves from Africa.

There were a lot of Epiphytes high up in the trees hanging many feet down from the branches, including a form of Harrisii which had been in flower during the night, probably as a pinky white, since the dead flower was very long and a maroon pink. On some trees, Rhipsalis hung down in huge clusters, usually from the top branches of very tall trees.

We had seen quite a number of Epiphytes in the mountains and on the north coast, but it was on the road running out beyond the airport to Port Royal that we were once again to find cacti in considerable numbers. Coming into Kingston, we saw tall hedges of Cereus and also Euphorbia triangularis with an occasional Opuntia Bergeriana with its red flower. Particularly on the peninsula, we found Cereus in large numbers, with a thin red stem and upright, not unlike Pachycereus Pringlei, when they were young but growing up into much smaller trees with far thinner branches. There were also Lemaireocereus hybrids, rather thicker in the stem, with a golden tip, and they were in flower. There were narrow Acanthocereus hybrids, and a lot of sprawling Opuntias with a yellow flower, growing, mostly very low and unkempt, in waste ground, a good deal of which is due for development.

**The author by a giant Pachycereus Pringlei
in Baja California. Note the tremendous
girth of the branches**

Ferocactus Acanthoides nestling amid the rocks

The Bahamas

The Great Exuma is a long and very narrow island, amid the dozens of other islands, many of them very small, which go to make the Exumas, about an hour's flight from Nassau. There is nothing but endless bush and you scarcely find a tree, except in George Town, which is really only a large village, with a magnificent harbour, and even there most of the trees are bent almost double by the prevailing wind. You find Agaves of the American species, some in flower, and also Furcraeas, in flower too with their shorter and thicker flower stems. There are a few Scillas on the islands and the same Euphorbia with a red flower which we had seen in the gardens of Trinidad. On the waste ground and in the small hamlets along the sea coast you find sprawling Opuntias, some with very fine long reddish brown spines, with the occasional yellow flower. Everywhere too, there are succulents of the Crassula and Sedum types, some with brownish bushes, some with a grey leaf, not unlike an Oscularia, up to three or four feet high, with a yellow flower. These succulents often grow within a few feet of the high tide and seem to flourish in the salt spray.

Venezuela

I flew to Carácas in Venezuela, where our Ambassador was most kind and gave me an introduction to Dr Lasser, a charming person who was professor of Botany at the Botanical Gardens. We set forth to the west at 7 am from Carácas, and although it was the dry season it rained for a lot of the day. We spent much time in the clouds which made photography difficult. Dr Lasser speaks English; Señor Braun, the head gardener there, speaks French, and our excellent driver, Phillippe, belonging to the air attaché at our Embassy, also speaks Spanish, so we made up a very competent party.

Throughout the day we saw cacti in large numbers, except when we crossed watersheds and ranges well over three thousand feet where there was dense, lush vegetation, obviously unsuitable for cacti. Despite the cloud and rain, it was always warm. We started in a village with a large number of Cereus griseus, whose fruit is good. This plant usually has narrow stems which fall all over the place, but sometimes they stay upright, branching from some three feet up the stem rather like a miniature edition of Pachycereus Pringlei. Nearby was the yellow flowering tree Cercidium procera. There were a few Cephalocereus Moritzianus, which we were to see in ever-increasing numbers, with their white heads, all the way to Coro. They are not so impressive as Euphorbia candelabra or Pachycereus Pringlei, nor were they as thick in the stems as Cephalocereus senilis.

There were some altogether better plants of Lemaireocereus deficiens growing alongside Opuntia caribeus, which is a Cholla cactus, which

was spreading everywhere. It has red berries. On the banks opposite there was a massive array of Aloe vera. All over the place there was Opuntia Wendtliana which, particularly in the hills around Coro, was growing over the ground like a carpet. It is fast ruining the countryside.

We motored on and found Pereskia guamacho with its leaves quite yellow to look at, because they have died off. We stopped by an old lady's shack to find a well-stocked smallholding, including pawpaws and avocado. There was the tall Furcraea geminispina, Acanthocereus Pentagonus, and even a small plant of Portulaca. At the roadside going over the hills, we saw the scarlet flowers of Ruellia fulgrans and, a little further on, some Rhipsalis, growing far up in a palm and quite impossible to reach, which was sad, as Señor Braun was collecting for us small plants of most things we saw.

Our host was careful as to where we stopped, as there are bandits who rob travellers, and we would have been a good subject for ransom, so he always had someone unostentatiously on the lookout. It is said that the bandits are paid by Russia and Cuba, and that they have to show results to prove that they are doing their job. Anyhow, we stopped again when we saw the narrow-stemmed Cephalocereus Schmidtianus over some rocks, and its big brother Cephalocereus Mortzianus standing on sentry behind. We stopped in a village and I photographed Furcraeas, which in these parts are growing in serried rows for sisal.

We had lunch near a bridge, where, in spate, the river overflowed and caused utter devastation several feet above the top of its bank. We stopped as there were some magnificent Cephalocereus Moritzianus, and then we saw the first of what turned out to be twenty Melocactus cæsinus, with their white Cephalium on their heads and in some cases a long pink seed pod. We looked everywhere for Mammillarias, as Señor Braun had once found some in these parts, but at the place he remembered it was too wet to move much off the roadside. Here we also found Jatropha urens, for all the world like a Euphorbia. There was also a big bush of Opuntia elatior, with its bigger leaves. It was a great day despite the rain, and on our way to our hotel we made a detour to see the vast sand dunes at Coro, which stretch for literally miles and are several miles deep, with Euphorbias and Cereus stretching right out to the sea.

Next morning we started at 6 am. It was dark until nearly 7 am and not light enough to photograph properly for another hour. After some fifteen miles, we turned west off the main road along an unmetalled road, with some stones. It was wet after yesterday's rains and in some places almost washed away at the sides, but the stones seemed to stop us skidding. There was the occasional mud house, and one or two Land-Rovers or tractors passed, but it is an eerie land, as if visited by the wrath of God. The soil is bright red and the erosion has to be seen to be believed, as the ground is level on either side of the road, with continuous huge deep fissures, where the water must pour down in the flash floods. It is a land where nothing grows; we saw few birds and almost no animal life, an occasional goat and not even the usual donkey.

We found the sloughed outer skin of a rattlesnake and Dr Lasser thought he heard the noise of one rattling. We found the skeleton of a five-foot python, picked clean by birds presumably, as we saw a hawk fly off with a snake in its mouth.

We saw quite a few cacti, mostly Lemaireocereus deficiens, and Cereus griseus—on the whole small plants, and half of them dead. The ground was covered with pieces of low Opuntia Wendtliana, which we had seen the day before, growing as a carpet some one foot tall only, but today it was just small isolated plants and leaves lying everywhere. We found too a Melocactus. We finished off with a curious breakfast from the car; dry bread, a rather soapy cheese and some delicious local oranges!

We returned, after a few miles down this road, to the main road with the usual excellent fast tarmac, and for some miles there were Cereus with carpets of Opuntia and some Melocactus, growing among green trees and bushes in much more hospitable land. We drove three hundred miles to lunch in Carora, having by-passed Maracaibo, the big oil town by the sea. For some 150 miles there were few cacti; the ground was richer, and it was obviously a land of water. We saw some lovely trees, including the purple-flowering Longicarphus serito, and Cyclosarum, with its bright yellow bell flowers, each on the end of a stem. Then there was a most lovely yellow tree just covered with golden bloom, called Tabebuilla. It is most beautiful, and for a few miles the landscape was yellow with it.

Between Carora and Barquisimeto, some ninety miles, we ran into cacti again. It was a narrower road, and much of it over the lower and outer slopes of the northern tip of the Andes, so it was just one mass of curves, whereas in the morning we had travelled along a continuous, straight, flat road. To start with, we found Cephalocereus Moritziana and then mostly Cereus griseus and Lemarieocereus deficiens. There were quite a number of Melocactus, the older places Opunti Wendtliana was again a carpet, and we saw no other Opuntia. As we climbed over the hills towards Barquisimeto, the countryside became green and more dense with trees, sometimes a few Cereus but in the end mostly a green Agave, often in flower. It was significant to note that after the start yesterday we saw few Agaves.

It had been a very interesting two days, my first visit to South America; it is quite different from Mexico and the southern states of USA. The plants are smaller and they are less varied. In every area we went, we saw mostly the same plants as we saw at the start of the journey.

Cereus griseus growing in great numbers near Carácas in Venezuela

A Cereus in the desolate 'hotland' of north-western Venezuela

Making a collection

The enthusiast who wishes to start a collection has a wide selection of different groups of plants at his disposal. 'Shall I make it a general one, embracing the best specimens of any genera which attract me or interest me; or shall I specialize and try to collect—rather like a stamp collector—every plant that I can lay hands on of several particular genera?' The eventual choice will depend on his own character, on his knowledge of his hobby, on the size of his purse, on the time at his disposal, and on the type of greenhouse or other accommodation which he possesses and the heating system available.

The beginner is well advised to start with plants that are comparatively easy to grow, and fortunately there is a good variety of interesting and attractive succulents which comes under this heading. It is a good plan to start with a wide variety, as by doing so it is possible to learn from the outset something about the culture of a representative collection.

An arrangement of cacti and succulents planted in shallow compost as a guide to help and encourage beginners

120

On pages 50-83 of this book there are specially-taken photographs of some fifty plants recommended as suitable to start a general collection, including a wide range of cacti, succulents and Epiphytes. It is not meant to be by any means a comprehensive list. There are many other suitable varieties which are comparatively easy to grow—but I have chosen a mixture of plants, some of which will flower and some of which are particularly interesting or have striking shapes. Some of these plants need different treatment from others, and this I hope will help to teach beginners, especially, how best to cope with various species.

For easy-flowering plants that bloom in the spring, I recommend red and yellow Rebutias, which are some of the earliest flowering; many Mammillarias flower in the spring and I suggest zeilmanniana for a good mauve and bocasana and wildii as good creams. Mammillaria elongata is also a decorative plant and often flowers well. Some Notocacti such as concinnus flower well, and Leninghausii is an interesting plant for any collection, though it usually does not flower till it is several years old. Chamæcereus silvestrii flowers

A lovely specimen of Rebutia senilis, with its flower-spines coming up from the bottom of the plant, as in all Rebutias

Rebutia miniscula (Aylostera)

A group of Gymnocalycium in flower

freely and is a decorative plant. The Gymnocalyciums and the Parodias have lovely big flowers and bloom in the early summer. Lobivias flower about the same time. In the later summer, you get Mammillaria kewensis, which is quite a good flowerer. The Echinopsis shoot out their lovely long flower stems and Hamatocactus setispinus and Crassula falcata flower well. In the autumn, you get Faucarias in flower, followed in the winter by Zygocactus königerweihnachtsfreude, which is succeeded by Zygocactus truncatus (the Christmas Cactus). In the New Year, the first plants to flower do so in late February and March (northern latitudes)–Echeveria Worfield Wonder is an admirable pot flower as its flowers are always dwarf, with it you can have Aeonium Haworthii and Bryophylium Fedschenkoi. Some of the first spring flowerers are the Schlumbergeras, which usually flower between Easter and Whitsun, with their long, tapering leaves and flowers. They are followed by the Epiphyllums, plants which are dull most of the year, but really are glorious when they have their lovely big flowers of all hues and shades.

For all the Epiphytes, including Epiphyllum, Zygocactus and Schlumbergeras, I suggest a slightly richer compost than the John Innes No. 2 which I use for all cacti and succulents. Some people add a little sand for their stone plants.

A plant which flowers most of the year is the Christ's Thorn (Euphorbia splendens), both in red and yellow. It hails from Madagascar and should not be exposed to frost. Sometimes you have Trichocereus spachianus in bloom with its lovely great white scented flowers, but it does not usually flower till it is some height. If you have a greenhouse I strongly recommend Selenicereus grandiflora, which will soon climb up upright and spread across the roof, with masses of lovely scented white flowers. If you have Stapelia veriegata, it may come out with its lovely, star-shaped big flower, but remember that it has a foul smell.

Now to discuss other plants, which are not so likely to flower soon. All will flower eventually, but many have to be some age before they do so. Let us deal with the tall plants first, which are so useful in any display or in miniature gardens. Crassula portulacea is a very strong plant and grows high and bushy, and is to my mind the best of all background plants. Other very useful ones are the Cereii, including Cereus peruvianus monstrosus with its rugged body. Euphorbia candelabra, with its lovely shapes, is a strong grower. The colourful Aeonium arborgeum and the tall, white easy-branching Cleistocactus strausii are very useful, as also the Prickly Pears, mostly strong, tough growers that spread quickly. Opuntia microdasys, which is a more delicate plant, is very attractive in white, yellow and red.

A group of Gymnocalycium, including Venturianum

Mammillaria Wildii

Lobivia Marsoneri in flower

123

**Left: Opuntia in flower in a garden on the
Costa Brava, Spain
Below: An Opuntia hedge
Opposite: Euphorbia Tananarive** see page 63

Let us look next at the plants that spread laterally, the Agaves, especially the gay green-and-yellow Agave americana variegata, and some of the Aloes of which Aloe variegata is very attractive. We have too the Barrel Cacti such as Ferocactus, and the glorious gold Echinocactus Grusonii, with its vicious spines, known rather unkindly as 'Mother-in-Law's Chair'. There are the ground cover plants in Crassula lycopodioides and Harrisia tortuosa, an ungainly, straggly plant which can, however, burst into lovely, white-scented flowers.

We now come to the interesting plants, some of which are more expensive, but which lend tone and sophistication to any collection. They are also attractive and decorative in their own ways. Cephalocereus senilis, the 'Old Man's Head'; the white Espostoa lanata; the white Kleinia tomentosa; the gaily marked Haworthia margaretifera; Kleinia neriifolia that grows like a palm tree; Oreocereus celsianus or trollii, the frilly-edged Cotyledon undulata; Senecio stapeliiformis with its attractive markings and often with a red flower. Lastly we come to the small Mesembryanthemums and the Stone Plants: Euphorbia obesa; the tiny Titanopsis; the Fenestrarias with their tiny windows; Astrophytum myriostigma, the 'Bishop's Cap'; and the mauve-coloured Cheiridopsis candidissima, and finally the Lithops, the 'Living Stones' and the tiny Conophytums.

A non-specialist collection

Some collectors, once out of the beginner stage, decide to continue to collect plants of any genera in which they think they will be interested. They have the world at their feet—quite literally—and costs and space are their only limits. There is much to be said for a general collection; specialization may lead you along a narrow, and rather stifling path.

It may well lead on to an unending quest for plants which can only be got at prices which you can ill afford, and may result in a rather miserable collection which, though technically interesting, consists of plants which it is well nigh impossible to get to grow strongly and healthily under the cultural conditions normally available in northern climates.

In specialist collections you will often find, too, that a rather miserable-looking plant, which happens to be difficult to find and possibly even more difficult to grow, is the ewe lamb and show-piece of the collection—in preference to a healthy-looking, free-flowering hybrid, which might well be the pièce de resistance in a general collection. But the non-specialist collector has none of these troubles. He is fettered by no inhibitions. Species and hybrid are all the same to him provided that he likes them and they fill a gap in his collection. He can pick and choose what plants he likes best, and as there are over 9000 different ones, his powers of selection are as good as infinite.

Echinopsis hybrid in full flower

Echinopsis in flower

Some of the recommended plants with which
to start a collection. These specimens, grown
in the author's gardens at Worfield, are
illustrated and described individually on
pages 50–83

**A magnificent old Ferocactus ingens near
Pachuca in Mexico**

In the build-up of a non-specialist collection, one of the important things to do is to seize every opportunity to collect any plant of a genus which you do not already possess. Catalogues and books and journals naturally help, and from these and travel articles you will learn the names of genera with which you are not familiar. You can then look these up and see if you think they are worthy of your collection. You need not limit yourselves to succulents but it is wise, I suggest, to limit your collection to the Xerophytic plants which can withstand drought conditions. I think it is also important in the unspecialist collection to realize that there is no need to replace anything that dies. To go further than that, you need never keep a plant that does not look well or will not do well for you. If you stick relentlessly to some plan of this sort, you will build up a collection of strong and healthy plants which will be a real pride to yourself and the envy of your friends and visitors.

For specialized collectors

Now we must consider the large number of people who nevertheless wish to specialize in the collection of certain particular genera. They have a wide and interesting selection from which they can make their choice. They have, too, an excellent opportunity to learn all about the plants of their choice and to become real experts on their cultivation.

A fascinating and very satisfying type of collection can be made from plants that will flower in northern climes with comparative ease. A heated greenhouse is, of course, of great help, and plants flower freely there, but it is quite possible to make them bloom in a living-room facing the sun. There is the added interest of trying to keep a few plants in flower all the year round. It is quite possible to do so, as you will have seen in the flowering varieties recommended for a collection at the start of this chapter.

Mammillarias are a fascinating genus, as the plants are so symmetrical and neat. Most of them will bloom freely every year in their attractive rings of mauve, pink or cream flowers, and they are small and will fit conveniently into a limited space. There are over 250 recognised species, most of which come from Mexico, as well as a number of hybrids. The flowers last for a week or more and new ones follow successively, so that it is possible to have rings of flowers on the plants for several weeks. Some species such as Mammillaria prolifera, Mammillaria texana, Mammillaria elegans and Mammillaria Schmollii have attractive red seed pods, which often stay long enough on the plant to encircle the next year's ring of flowers.

Epiphyllums and their relations make another attractive and interesting collection. It is possible to have a blaze of colour in the spring with all shades of white, cream, pink, orange and purple,

Mammillaria Sheldonii in bloom with its lovely large flowers

Schlumbergera in flower at Worfield

Mammillaria elongata in flower

Zygocactus Königer-Weihnachtsfreude in flower. A very strong grower

Zygocactus truncatus: the 'Christmas Cactus' in flower

Kalanchoë Mauganii

whilst in the winter months there can be continuous colour in the house from the various kinds of Zygocactus. Some Epiphyllums, too, will bloom in the Autumn. These plants will do well in darker houses than the desert cacti and succulents and can stand out in the garden from the end of May frosts to the start of the September ones.

Lithops and Conophytums For the average collector with limited space and time at his disposal, it may be wise, at the start at any rate, to limit his collection to these two basic genera, though there are some people who limit themselves still further, to a collection of one or the other. There is a large number of species in both, many of which are difficult to identify even by collectors of great experience, and a complete study of them would be a fascinating occupation. Both genera flower freely, and do so at different times of the year, just as they do in their own homelands in South Africa, where they get their annual rains at completely different times.

Crassulas The smaller Crassulas, which are most attractive and sometimes very difficult to propagate, like Crassula columnaris, Crassula pyramidalis, Crassula tecta, Crassula anomala, Crassula Gillii, Crassula arta, Crassula deltoidea, Crassula deceptrix and Crassula barbata, to name just a few of them, would make an interesting collection. These members of the Crassula genus could be collected on their own or they might be combined with a few of the following selected plants from the Mesembryanthemum family which flower freely and are of special interest: Didymaotus lapidiformis, with its attractive shining white and pink flowers blooming on two spikes which stick out of its tiny bulbous body; the Fenestrarias, the little window plants; Frithia pulchra, with its deep purple flower; Muiria hortenseæ, with its very succulent green body; Muiria gibbæum, the rare hybrid of Muiria hortenseæ and gibbæum album; Pleiospilos prismaticus which thrives in bright sunshine and can be found in clumps of bright crimson; Rhinephyllum Muiria with its fascinating little pink flower; Trichodiadema densum and Trichodiadema barbatum with their attractive mauve flowers. To these can be added other rarities, such as the Adeniums, which are very difficult to grow; a variety of the tiny Anacampseros, the Bulbine, with its little yellow flower hardly showing above ground; the interesting Fockea from the Karoo, which is usually well-nigh buried; some rare varieties of Hoodia, the long flask-shaped Pachypodium from Namaqualand and Testudinaria with its long clambering leaf stems.

There are, of course, other collections which can be made, either alone or by collecting two or more of the other collections. These include Rebutias, Notocacti, Gymnocalyciums, Opuntias, Gibbæums, Kalanchoes and the Mesembryanthemum family.

Some hints on arranging a collection
The earlier part of this book depicted the way of life of cactus and succulent plants in their own native habitats. My descriptions of the countryside in which they live were intended to give an idea of how the plants fit into this landscape. It is sometimes possible to see arrangements of these plants in naturalistic surroundings at some of the larger horticultural shows, where they may measure some forty feet by ten feet. Most of these exhibits combine the cacti from America with the succulents from Africa, since it is more difficult to arrange a really big exhibit with only American plants, there being too few American succulents with which to soften the effect of the desert cacti and give the display light and shade. Moreover, you would need to have very big plants to make a worthwhile picture, unless you decided to give it additional artificial aids, either with painted background or with fluorescent or floodlights. These effects, however, can be very expensive, and in the non-competitive classes, care has to be taken not to shake the susceptibilities of the judges, who are sometimes not too sympathetic to radical changes in ideas. There is, however, I am glad to say, a growing tendency towards new ideas in the presentation of stands and many foreign firms are leading the way with attractive new schemes.

As a result of this development, popular opinion is swinging in the direction of exhibits in which the plants are laid out as if they are either in a garden or in the natural conditions of their own homeland.

Arrangements in greenhouses
I am assuming now that you have a greenhouse or conservatory with some form of heating, at least sufficient to keep out the frost, and that you are one of a number of collectors who prefer to show off their plants to their friends in some arrangement akin to the way in which they grow in their own homelands. This can be quite easily done with whatever size plants you have. If they are smallish, then the arrangement can be made on the staging. In this case I would have the compost only about three inches deep at the most. I find that small arrangements like this thrive and grow extremely well in a shallow compost. Some form of surround will be required with which to retain the peat, sand or soil which you use. To make an attractive display it will be advisable to vary the contours of the ground. This can be done partly with the help of pieces of rock. Tufa is a good type, as it is full of holes rather like pumice stone and is attractive to look at. The holes can also be enlarged so that plants can be grown in them. Tufa is full of valuable minerals and plants root themselves far into the rock and grow very well.

Higher ground can also be made by raising some of the plants on bricks or rubble. If you do not wish to use a great deal of peat or soil, then rubble and sand can be used to fill in between the plants. The whole effect can be finished off with different coloured chippings, which can either be mixed or put on in succession to get the final colouring required.

If the collection is a large one and has a number of tall or broad plants, the display will have to be set out on the floor. For a first attempt, I would suggest something like an area of twelve feet by six feet. (You will usually need a depth of at least six feet, as it is difficult to arrange a very narrow display.) It will be wise at the start to make either a small model or a scale drawing of the proposed layout. By doing so it is often possible to improve the design and to lessen the chance of making unnecessary mistakes. It is important to have this model or drawing on the site when work is started and to measure out the distance with string and pegs on the ground to be covered.

The first thing to do is to lay out the high ground, to dig any ravines or streams and to erect any huts or bridges. Bricks or larger pieces of stone or concrete will assist in making the high ground, and the steeper sides can be made with sandbags filled with soil, sand or peat. The rocks must next be placed in position, and it is most important that they should be arranged in accordance with their natural strata. The correct side of the rock must be uppermost, with all rock facing in the same direction and tilting at the same angle—if possible, in a striking manner that will help to dominate the 'landscape'. If there is a painted background, the rocks should be arranged so that they merge into it, while its colour should resemble that of the rocks, and the colour of the finishing chippings should be as nearly as possible the same as that of the background.

The bigger plants should then be put in, as they will act as pointers for the subsequent arrangment. They can either be set into the landscape in their pots or they can be knocked out of their pots and planted in the compost. In the latter case, they will have their root action free in the compost and many plants, particularly such genera as Aloes, Agaves, Kalanchoes and Opuntias, will grow more freely and more quickly than they would in pots.

There should be a plan for the general arrangement of the plants. They can be grouped by colours or by types. The former is the most attractive but the latter may be more instructive. If you are interested in colour, you can have white, gold, red and light green groups. In the white ones, for instance, you can include Cleistocactus strausii, Oreocereus, Espostoa lanata, Cephalocereus senilis, Notocactus haselbergii, Notocactus scopa, Mammillaria hahniana and Mammillaria geminispina, You can make most attractive groups in this way, including in the golden one some Echinocactus grusonii and Notocactus leninghausii.

It is important to try to give distance and perspective to the layout, and with this in view some of the larger plants can be placed towards the front of the arrangement whilst some striking little plants such as a low Prickly Pear or an Opuntia exaltata cristata can be made to peer over rock faces at the back of the picture, in positions where they merge into the backcloth.

Along the front and sides of the model, some of the small plants can be arranged in groups. For instance the small Pebble Plants can be placed very attractively in one group, which will be full of interest. These groups can either be at ground level, or mounted on some form of rock plateau, with the plants buried in peat and finished off with small pebbles and stones. Any pots which are not already concealed can be hidden with large pieces of bark, after which the gaps between the plants can be covered with peat and chippings. Some parts of the display may have to be perfected quite early in the proceedings if they are in positions that will be difficult to reach afterwards without upsetting the work already done.

Paths must be kept through the layout for the purposes of watering, tending plants and for the benefit of those wishing to take photographs. These paths can be finished off with stones and rather larger chippings, so as to give them a natural appearance and one that is different to the surrounding terrain.

Collecting without a greenhouse

There are many people who have no greenhouse and who have no prospect of getting one; or who are not allowed by their local authorities to erect one. To them I say, do not be down-hearted: you too can keep succulent plants. It is quite possible to have the pleasure of a collection of them in your house or flat or lodgings—and your limit is chiefly the whim and the will of your wife or mother or housekeeper or lodging-house keeper! If you are untrammelled by any of these, you can house a limitless collection on tables, windows ledges, sinks or shelves, but it is important to remember that the plants which you can keep in a sun-facing window, with all the light you can give them, will do best. There are, I am glad to say, thousands of collectors and enthusiasts who keep a small collection in pots in rooms and who take the greatest interest in collecting and tending their plants. Possibly they live in a city and can have no garden or allotment, but with these plants in their rooms they are able to indulge their innate love of a garden. Moreover, when they go away for a holiday, these plants will stand up to neglect far better than others, for it is a well-known fact that succulents thrive better on neglect than they do on pampering and overwatering.

A miniature garden, including Echeverias,
Opuntia cylindrica cristate and Crassulas,
with Cereus pachypodium longifolia and
Crassula portulacea as background plants

Miniature gardens

I believe there is yet further scope for thousands, even tens of thousands of people who are not particularly interested in making a collection of succulents and yet who are fascinated, interested and amused by them and who want to enjoy the pleasure of growing them and watching them come to maturity and flower. They are more intrigued by the beauty of the plants, or by the interest in arranging them together in some form of garden, than they are in forming them up like soldiers in serried rows. For them, there is pleasure to be had from a miniature garden which they can keep quite happily in their house or flat. These can be bought at all prices, with three or four plants in the smaller ones, and up to twenty or thirty in the larger ones. Often they consist only of succulents which are gayer in colour and cheaper to produce than cacti.

The essential point to realise about these gardens is that they consist of living plants used for decorative purposes and that therefore they must always be kept looking fresh and green. This means that they must have some water all the year round. It is easiest to look after them in a heated greenhouse where they get ample light and so can be given plenty of water, but if you take a little trouble they can be made to do equally well in a living-room. If the room has central heating, they will require plenty of water – in fact, the warmer the house the more water they want. A sun-facing window is ideal, for if they do not have ample light many of the plants, particularly those with berry-like leaves, will get drawn and will eventually die, others will turn yellow and get long, lanky and unsightly. It is essential, too, not to allow them to get frosted in a window in very cold weather.

Whatever happens do not keep them permanently at the back of a room on a sideboard, bookshelf or mantelpiece, and, if you use them as a table centre, move them frequently over to the window for light. If you can put them out for a spell in the summer, after the frosts are over, they will benefit tremendously and will repay you amply for your care and trouble on their behalf.

If you would prefer to make these gardens yourself, you can most certainly do so. The first thing to decide is what kind of container to put the plants in. There is always a controversy about using porous or glazed ones. Each has its advantages, but after a great deal of experience of both kinds, I have come to the conclusion that succulent plants flourish equally well in either of them. There are those who profess to have little faith in glazed dishes or bowls, as they have no drainage, but to my mind this type of container conserves moisture better than the porous ones and, provided that it is never allowed to become waterlogged by over-watering, it gives the plants a long lease of healthy, vigorous life.

You may decide to build a very big one like an Alpine garden in a porous or a glazed sink. These are usually fairly deep and I would suggest that you put a good deal of drainage material, such as crocks, turf or stones, at the bottom of the sinks before you fill them up with compost. For the medium-sized garden, there are many useful types of containers: round and oval copper dishes, large pottery roasters and decorative pottery bowls in varying shapes, round, rectangular and oval. You can sometimes also find containers which give the effect of a Cotswold dry-stone wall. For smaller gardens, you have the use of all kinds of containers, porous, glazed, plastic or wood. It is a matter of choice. Children can amuse themselves with tiny containers possibly two or three inches in diameter and an inch to an inch and a half deep, in which with the help of a tiny piece of rock and two or three small plants, they can make up a decorative little garden arrangement.

For all my gardens, I use John Innes No. 2 compost, without drainage crocks. If you want to make up gardens consisting of Lithops and other mimicry types of Mesembryanthemum, I suggest that you will do best to concentrate these together in one garden. Tufa rock makes a good background for them and you might plant some of them in the crevices, where they may do well, as they like a well drained position.

The next problem is whether to mix cacti and succulents or whether to concentrate only on one or the other. In many ways the mixed bowl is the most intriguing and can often be made the most attractive. It contains all the softness in shade and shape of the succulents and at the same time there can be a tall blue Opuntia robusta to relieve the picture and to remind one that the Prickly Pear of Western locations really does exist in miniature. The disadvantage of the mixed type of garden mainly concerns watering: the succulents need plenty of water and some cacti will rot at the stem if they get too much. But there are luckily some cactus plants, such as Opuntia robusta and Cereus peruvianus which are very tough and will stand up to the damper conditions which the succulents enjoy.

For a mixed bowl you have a wide range of plants. For the background, there are Opuntia robusta, Opuntia vulgaris or any other strong Opuntia. There are many strong Cerei, perhaps particularly Cereus peruvianus and Cereus Jamacaru and Cereus peruvianus monstrosus. Also, there is the excellent strong Crassula portulacea with its waxen leaves – a 'must' in any arrangement.

For the centre of the bowl, there are Cleistocactus Strausii, Espostoa lanata, Trichocereus, Aloes, Crassula falcata, Aeonium Haworthii, Lycopoidiodes, faucarias and Echinocactus Grusonii. For the front of the bowl there are many good varieties – Cheiridopsis candidissima, Rebutias,

135

Notocactus and Chamæcereus silvestrii and Crassula Schmidtii, (a good autumn flowerer). Last, but not least, there are the Mammillarias. I would not use the hairy ones, as they may rot off. But there are many excellent varieties—elongata, ruffo crocea with its red seed pods, kewensis which flowers late in the year, Wildii or Wildii cristata, just to mention a few.

Then there is the garden which consists of cacti only. It is difficult to make this look attractive if the plants are small, but with larger plants you can arrange a lovely bowl, particularly if you choose plants of different colour and shade. The large green Cereus, the tall slender white Cleistocactus Straussii, the round golden Notocactus Lening-hausii, the red Thelocactus bicolor and, of course, the common Prickly Pear will do well. You can also include the dwarfer easy-flowering varieties such as Chamaecereus silvestrii, with its trumpet-shaped scarlet flower, the many Rebutias with red and pink flowers and Rebutia Marsoneri with its yellow flower. Then there are the many easy-flowering Mammillarias such as kewensis with its purple flower, Wildii and multiceps with their cream flowers.

There is the large range of Notocactus, Lobivias and Gymnocalyciums, all of which will flower well. These gardens are more expensive in original outlay, but they will last a long time and will stand up better than the succulents to a darker room.

Now for succulent bowls, of which an immense variety can be made up; plants of every height, shape and shade of colour can be included and most of them require about the same amount of water. They are not expensive to buy when they are small and as they grow larger they can be pruned in order to maintain their shape and correct size in the garden. The cuttings that you take can be used for further gardens and you will find it most interesting to root them and grow them on. All succulent gardens require plenty of light and should never be left in a dark corner, or under a shelf. They prefer sunlight, like plenty of water and must never be allowed to get frosted.

There are tall plants for the background such as the strongly-growing Crassula portulacea, with broad, darker green leaves which turn a russet red colour in full sunlight. It will easily grow up to eighteen inches in height in the bigger types of

Cheiridopsis candidissima

miniature garden. As a medium-sized plant, there is Crassula lycopoidiodes, with its tall, slender stems, available in several varieties with different shades of green, until one comes to the variegated form with its lovely mauvish-grey stems. Cheiridopsis candidissima, with its pale blue leaves shaded with mauve, is another attractive and serviceable plant, and so is Sedum Adolphii with its beige-coloured berry-like leaves, which is a particularly useful foil to the more usual green-coloured plants. For the small parts of the garden, most of the Sempervivums are good, while of the flowering plants, Crassula Schmidtii, with its red and sometimes white flowers, keep its blooms over a long period. Crassula falcata is a useful plant which can flower well, and any of the stronger-growing Aloes do well, as also do the Faucarias.

This is but a small selection of the various plants available for combination. But I hope that I have whetted your appetite as to the attraction and interest which can be added to the decor of your house by a miniature garden in which cacti and succulents have been artistically arranged.

Crassula portulacea

Aloe variegata

Lobivia Marsoheri in flower

Conophytum in flower

Fenestraria

A group of Gymnocalycium in flower

Lophophora

Opuntia hybrid

Care and cultivation

The early sections of this book will have given you some idea of the conditions under which cacti and succulent plants grow in the wild in their own homelands. We are now going to deal with the care and propagation of these plants in our own countries. Succulent plants *can* exist naturally for a long time without water, but at the end of a long drought they look shrivelled up and black, and very few people would welcome plants in this state in their collection at home. So the problem is how best to keep our plants looking healthy and strong throughout the year, without letting them lose their characteristics. An important thing to realise is that the majority of succulent plants love sunshine and fresh air—and therefore, particularly if we live in a dull or foggy climate, we should try to give them as much light and air as possible. If you are keeping them in a living-room, they prefer a sun-facing window. If you cannot give them that, then try to give them a spell out of doors, during the spring and

An excellent picture of the tall and unexpected seed-pod of Stapelia variegata, illustrating the care that will have to be taken to avoid the seed bursting all over the place

summer. If you do this, remember to put them in a place that is safe from children, cats, dogs and birds.

How and when to water our plants is quite a problem. In general, succulents are said to thrive on neglect. They are therefore very satisfactory plants for the owner of a small house who wants to leave them unattended, without a 'baby-sitter', when he goes on holiday. This does not mean that they can be neglected throughout the year—or just given some water when you think of it. The amount of water they want and the frequency at which they need it depends partly on the climate and the time of the year and partly on the heat of the place in which they are kept. Many cacti, especially large show plants, prefer a resting period in the winter, which corresponds roughly with periods of drought in their own country. For instance, my own large show plants at Worfield in England are very seldom, if ever, watered between November and March. This means, too, that the greenhouses can be kept at a low temperature in the winter, such as 4·4 to 10·0 degrees centigrade, which is also economical in fuel.

The small cacti need some water during the winter, particularly in warm greenhouses and living rooms, but it is best only to water them on fine days when there is some sunshine and on days that are unlikely to be followed by a sharp frost. Such plants enjoy a slightly higher temperature—say 10·0 to 12·8 degrees centigrade. Succulents need some water in the winter, in the same way as small cacti. Bowl gardens need more regular watering, as they consist of a floral arrangement which you hope will grow well and look flourishing for you all the year round. When spring comes, all your plants want plenty of water till about the end of October. If the weather is hot, you may water four or five times during the week. It is usually best to water overhead, to ensure that each pot in its turn is well filled with water. In the early days of spring you must ensure that your pots get properly soaked, to ensure that the water gets right down to the roots. If you have a large collection it is quite alright to water with a rose on the end of a hosepipe. You can, of course, dip the pots in water and let the water ooze to the top. This may be wise especially with the larger plants in the early spring, but if you do soak them in this way, remember that it is very easy to leech away the soluble food in your compost. Anyhow, remember to give your plants plenty of water, and do not be tempted to dribble water on to them with a small can or teapot.

Compost

I use John Innes No. 2 compost for all my cacti and succulents. It is an easy compost to work, feeds the plants well and helps to give them good drainage. You can, of course, use a slightly more

141

sandy compost for Lithops and a slightly richer compost for Epiphytes, but I find that one way and another John Innes No. 2 is a good all-round compost for work with all these plants. When potting-up, remember that the white milky liquid in Euphorbias can give you trouble if it gets into your eyes or mouth or cuts—so wash your hands after you have potted up Euphorbias. A few Euphorbias are poisonous, such as Virosa, which the American Indians used to use for their poisoned arrows—but otherwise succulents are not in any way poisonous. However, if you do get cactus spines stuck into you, do your best to pull them out cleanly, as a broken stump in your hand can fester like a rose thorn.

If you are potting-up Epiphyllums, remember that in their own lands they live mostly up in the jungle trees, with their leaves hanging pendant so that the water drains off them all the time. This warns us that they always need excellent drainage. Do not be tempted to give them too much nitrogen in any fertiliser or they will become overlush and green on the leaves at the expense of having good flowers, which, after all, is why we keep them.

Propagation

There are two principal means of propagation, by seed sowing and by vegetative propagation (or 'cuttings'). In their desert homes, the majority flower, fruit and seed. The seeds drop on the ground or are carried elsewhere by wind, rodent or bird. The rains come, the seeds germinate and those that survive grow into healthy plants. Some plants (such as Opuntias) propagate freely from pads and offsets, while Sedums and other plants with small leaves like berries, drop them all over the ground, where they root and quickly grow into plants.

Electric soil-warming beds are very useful and enable one to start propagation in plenty of time. Soil warming also adds to the general warmth of the greenhouse—but beware not to seal your house completely with polythene, or an undue level of humidity will build up inside it.

Commercial firms with bottom heat start sowing early in the new year, but for the amateur with no soil warming I would not suggest sowing before April or May. Fill a shallow pan or tray with John Innes seed compost, slightly moistened. Sieve a little ordinary compost on top of it and tamp it down with a piece of wood. With large seeds like Opuntias, sprinkle the seeds well apart, and cover thinly with chippings. With very small seeds, sprinkle the chippings before you sow. Remember to put in a label. Place a glass sheet over the pan, and cover it with brown paper. Turn the glass each day to avoid condensation. As the seeds start to germinate, remove the paper and raise the glass a little each day. Never let your seedlings grow leggy. Then prick out your seedlings into a pan of John Innes No. 2, using something like a mapping pen with the nib blunted to dig the holes and lift the

seedlings in.

Vegetative propagation

Now we come to vegetative propagation. It is best to take cuttings in the spring and summer, as they grow so slowly in the winter. A clean cut is made at the base of each cutting. This is laid on a shelf for a few days to callous over, forming a skin over the wound. The cutting can be rooted quickly in sand or vermiculite, but this is very barren—and commercial growers often use half sand and half loam, in which the cutting can live happily for a few weeks, in case they do not have a chance to pot the cutting as soon as it is rooted. If you take cuttings off tall Cereus or Euphorbias, remember that the parent plant will at first be unsightly with the naked cut, as the new shoot will never come up in the middle. It will shoot up along the side of the stem where the sap is running strongest. But in all probability it will branch out in two or three new shoots, which will eventually look quite good. Some Sedums and Echeverias propagate both from cuttings and berries. Lay the berry down on some compost. Do not bury the end of the berries, and do not water them till the rosettes are rooted. Some plants like Crassula Schmidtii are propagated by division, like ordinary garden plants.

Grafting cacti

Cacti can also be propagated by grafting. This is a common practice on the European continent, particularly in Holland and Belgium, where the large light windows of the houses usually contain a fine array of pot plants. In these countries the main requirement in succulents is for large and showy ones to make a display in their windows. Grafting enables cacti to grow more quickly, just as a hybrid rose will grow more readily on a briar stock, and it is for this reason that you find so many grafted plants in these countries. In the USA, collectors use grafts to make slow-growing plants grow on more quickly, and particularly to make hybrids with which to improve American flowering plants, though not so freely as is done in Holland.

In England, grafting is not popular, since the many enthusiastic collectors in the country prefer to let their plants grow on their own roots as they do in their countries of origin; they fear that grafting will distort the growth of their plants and cause them to become drawn and over-lush.

I have found grafting useful for hanging and drooping plants such as Aporocactus and Zygocactus. You can produce more effective specimen plants by the use of grafts which enable the plant to make full value of its pendant habits. In the case of Zygocacti, which grow during the winter months, it is advisable to use a stock such as Selenicereus Macdonaldiæ or Harrisii Martinii, which are also winter-growing plants. A cleft graft is a useful one to use for these plants. Cut the stock off horizontally at the top and then with a sharp knife cut it into a V-shaped slit about an inch deep. Then taper off the scion, insert it into the cleft and fix it there with an Opuntia spine. Provided that the graft is done quickly and at a time when the sap of both plants is running, the two pieces will quickly join. After the graft is completed, keep the soil moist, but be careful not to water at all for a few days in case the water should run down on to the graft and prevent the two pieces from joining. If the cactus spine later appears to be unsightly, cut it at both ends when the plant is firm and the junction is calloused over.

Pests and diseases

Fortunately for collectors, cacti and succulents are very tough. They stand up to rough treatment very well. They can be taken to shows under conditions that might make other plants irretrievably damaged. If you go away on holiday for two or three weeks, you can leave your plants without anyone to look after them. But, on the other hand, it is important to remember that pests and diseases more readily take control when plants are over-dry. It is important to watch your plants carefully and stop any trouble at its inception. Furthermore, cleanliness is very important in the area where you keep your plants, be it in the house or in a green-house. Unswept corners with broken plants, pieces of paper and old soil can harbour pests and diseases, which can attack your plants and give you a lot of trouble.

Mealy Bug

This is the best-known pest and the one most likely to attack succulents. The insects are small and covered with a white woolly secretion. They make nests with this woolly material, in which they lay their eggs. They are not active during cold weather, and they come to life with sudden renewed activity in the spring. If you can spot them at once and you have just a small collection, you can often pick them off with a pin. If you have a more serious infection, use some proprietory pest destroyer which calls itself a mealy bug killer.

If you have a big collection, it is best to use one of the 'systemic' insecticides which are available under various proprietary names in different parts of the world. The active ingredients of each kind which you should look for in the 'small print' on the containers are the following: *demeton-S-methyl*; *oxydemeton-methyl*; *demeton*; *malathion* and *diazinon* (which controls red spider, scale insects and mushroom flies in addition to mealy bug).

Remember that an insecticide needs careful handling: it is wise to use rubber gloves and a nose pad and to be careful not to get it into your eyes, nose or a cut. It is best to water it in with a rosed watering can or spray. It has an unpleasant smell, but this does not matter as it clears itself in a short time. As this is a chemical which is taken up *via* the plant roots into its sap, it is no use using it except at times of the year when the plants are growing and can absorb it. Advice on the right preparation to use can be had from any good supplier of gardening chemicals. Collectors in Great Britain may find it useful to write to the Royal Horticultural Society (Wisley Gardens, Ripley, near Woking, Surrey) and ask for their excellent annotated list of approved pesticides for amateur gardeners.

Other pests

Scale can be a troublesome insect. It spreads quickly and forms a nasty looking hard crust over the plant. In small collections, you can sometimes remove it with a stiff brush, but for larger ones I should spray with a diazinon liquid, in the same way as dealing with mealy bug. Slugs can be very troublesome. Anti-slug and anti-snail preparations containing *metaldehyde*, laid out at intervals on small pieces of glass, should control it. Look out for aphis, black fly and white fly, which can damage a collection, and spray at once with a proprietary brand of pesticide. If you get a bad infection, you may have to fumigate the greenhouses.

Rot

The chief disease to attack succulents is due to some form of fungus which creates a squashy brown pulp just above ground level. This is often due to overwatering and bad drainage, when the roots cannot breathe and dampness collects round the stems. As soon as you spot this fungus, scrape it out carefully till all the soft material is removed and treat it with a little fine sulphur dust. Plants in transit sometimes get bruises and if you spot the bruise cut out the trouble and dust with sulphur.

Rot may set in if you have excessive condensation or drips from leaks in your greenhouse. Hairy plants such as Cephalocereus senilis, Oreocereus or Mammillaria Hahniana are very likely subjects for rot, and for these plants it is often wise to sprinkle coarse grit chippings over the top of the compost to keep the area round the collar of the plant as well drained and dry as possible.

Scorch

This can do damage to your plants and spoil the look of them. If the weather is very hot, it may be wise to put a paint wash over the greenhouse to mitigate the worst rays of the midday sun. In hot weather beware of watering your plants in the middle of the day. It is best to water either early in the morning or late in the evening. Finally, remember that cleanliness will save you from a lot of trouble. Fumigate your greenhouse at least once a year and at the same time wash down everything in the house—including glass, staging pipes and walls—with strong disinfectant, such as a liquid carbolic soap which is immediately soluble in water.

Saguaros of unusual shape near Tucson, Arizona